The Author

BESIDES COLLECTING and creating double-barreled definitions, Leonard Louis Levinson seems to have done a little bit of everything—from cleaning out the lions' cages with the Hagenbeck-Wallace Circus to dreaming up, in the space of eighteen hours, the characters, locale, format, and first script of "The Great Gildersleeve." He also thought up Fibber McGee's fabulous hall closet.

A native of Pittsburgh, Levinson received his formal education in his home town and in Portland, Oregon, San Diego, Los Angeles, and also at the Universities of Pittsburgh and California. He appeared as a sword-carrier in *The Merchant of Venice* in a production which starred Walter Hampden. At 22 he wrote and directed one of the world's swiftest "quickie" movies, "Pitfalls of Passion," which cost less than $4,000 and grossed $2,000,000. He has also written comedy lines uttered by comics on radio, television, phonograph records, and in the theater, night clubs, movies, and newspaper columns; sketches and lyrics for musicals; a number of screen plays.

The author of magazine fiction and mystery stories, Levinson says he literally has half a dozen cookbooks under his belt. Among his other works are *Wall Street: A Pictorial History; Caveman to Spaceman; Laugh It Off;* a one-volume version of *The Memoirs of Casanova* (Collier Books).

The Left Handed Dictionary

LEONARD LOUIS LEVINSON

COLLIER BOOKS, NEW YORK

COLLIER-MACMILLAN LIMITED, LONDON

FIFTH PRINTING 1966

Introduction

MANY YEARS AGO, when we were both working as reporters on *Variety*, in Hollywood, Ted Taylor, a man with some of the most varied and complete files in the world, showed me a number of index cards on which he had written wonderful definitions of his own composition. They were tart, tongue-in-cheek, opposite descriptions of words, reflecting his insight and views.

Now, there must be a hundred books which could be dredged out of Ted's files. This was the one about which I became enthusiastic. So enthusiastic, in fact, that I began coining and adding definitions of my own to his list. And Ted kept writing new ones, too.

As the years passed, the collection grew and we decided to have it published as a book. We enlarged its dimensions and combed literature, folk sayings, and the popular press for the best of definitions written by others. We made it into a game we played at parties. We collected amusing on-the-spur word meanings from friends. These new definitions and other contributions of writers we knew, made directly for this book, are indicated by an [*]. Every effort has been made to trace other collected definitions to their original sources, and where no definite credit can be given the attribution is to Anon., or his son (that clever little bastard) Anon., Jr.

As the result of receiving a set of paper napkins with Southern words and meanings by a friend passing through Charleston, S. C., the author began recording New Yorkese and will soon launch a lexicon of that somewhat bewildering language for the enlightenment of visitors to Manhattan. The New Yorkese definitions as well as all those which are uncredited are original ones.

Many of the latter appeared as a feature, "The Left-handed Dictionary," in *Cosmopolitan* over a period of eighteen months in the late 1940s and echoes have kept appearing in *Coronet* and *Reader's Digest,* as well as in many unauthorized sources. In fact, *The Left-Handed Dictionary* has been, until now, the most widely-quoted unpublished book in history.

About seven years ago, Ted Taylor found that there were other subjects in his files which engaged his attention more intently and since that time the author has gone on alone, gathering definitions and coining new ones. While humor changes, and many of the older definitions were discarded when they lost their meaning, almost all of Ted Taylor's coinage stand the test of time brightly. Since his was the original inspiration and since his contribution has been so substantial, I would like to dedicate this book

TO MY FRIEND

TED TAYLOR

THE
LEFT HANDED
DICTIONARY

A

A.A.A.A.A. An organization for drunks who drive.

*Martin Burden**

A.W.O.L. Rookie hooky.
—(Navy) A bolt from the blue. *Eleanor R. Merrill*

ABILITY. The art of getting credit for all the home runs that somebody else hits. *Casey Stengel*

ABLUTIONS. The art of washing without going bloolloolloolloollooll.

ABSCONDING. A sudden move to get rich.

ABSENT-MINDEDNESS. Searching for the horse you are riding.

Russian proverb

ABSTAINER. A person who can let anything but well enough alone.

ACADEMY AWARDS. A place where everyone lets off esteem.

Lou Brecker

ACAPULCO. A way of singing without musical accompaniment.

Joseph Pasternak

ACCIDENT. A surprise arranged by nature.
— A condition in which presence of mind is good, but absence of body better. *Foolish Dictionary*

ACCOMPLICE. The one who lacks brains as well as honesty.

ACCORDION. A bagpipe with pleats.

ACCURACY. The vice of being right.

ACHILLES. The boy whose mother dipped him in the River Stinx until he was intollerable. *Anon., Jr.*

9

ACORN. An oak in a nutshell.

ACQUAINTANCE. A friend who borrowed money from you.

ACRIMONY. Sometimes called holy, another name for marriage.
Anon., Jr.
— What a man gives his divorced wife.   *Anon., Jr.*

ACROPOLIS. The she-wolf that nursed Romeo and Juliet.
Anon., Jr.

ACTING. A sad business where you crawl from hope to hope.
Walter Slezak
— The moving picture of nature.   *William Winter, 1888*
— The lowest of arts.   *George Moore*
— An art which consists of keeping the audience from cough-
ing.   *Sir Ralph Richardson*

ACTOR. A man who can walk to the side of a stage, peer into
the wings filled with dust, other actors, stagehands, old
clothes and other claptrap, and say "What a lovely view
there is from this window."   *Variety*
— A man who makes faces for a living.
— A guy who steals towels.   *Harry Delmar*
— A puppet under its own power.
— A musician who plays on a homemade instrument—himself.
Helen Hayes
— A man with an infinite capacity for taking praise.
Michael Redgrave
— In Europe, an actor is an artist. In Hollywood, if he isn't
working, he's a bum.   *Anthony Quinn*
MOVIE ACTOR. A spook on a sheet.   *Richard Connell*
ACTORS. Casual laborers.   *Lillian Braithwaite*
ACTRESS. A woman who is still married to an actor.
MOVIE ACTRESS. Anybody who's got a dimple.
George M. Cohan

ADAGE. A proverb with long whiskers.

ADAGIO. A kind of anesthetic dancing.   *Anon., Jr.*

ADAM. The first man to tell anybody about his operation.
ADAM AND EVE. The Pilgrim Fathers.   *Anon., Jr.*

ADAM'S RIB. The original bone of contention.
Oliver Herford

ADHERENT. A follower who has not yet learned the truth.

ADJECTIVE. A word hanging down from a noun. *Anon., Jr.*

AD LIBBER. A man who stays up all night to memorize spontaneous jokes. *Wall Street Journal*

ADMIRAL. A general at sea.

ADOLESCENCE. The time when a boy stops collecting stamps and starts playing post office.
— The period in which the young suddenly feel a great responsibility about answering the telephone.
— The stage between puberty and adultery. *Anon., Jr.*

ADOPTION. Painless parenthood.

ADULT. One old enough to know better.
— One who has committed adultery.
— A man that has stopped growing at both ends but not in the middle. *Anon., Jr.*

ADULTERY. A matter of sofa. *Napoleon*
— Confusing the issue.

ADVANCE. To move along the line of most resistance.

ADVENTURE. A sign of incompetence. *Vilhjalmur Stefansson*
— Rightly considered, only an inconvenience.
G. K. Chesterton

ADVERB. An adjective with a tail on it.

ADVERTISE. To ring a bell in print.
ADVERTISEMENT. The most truthful part of a newspaper.
Thomas Jefferson, 1773
ADVERTISING. Something against nature. *Thomas Carlyle*
— Something which makes one think he's longed all his life for a thing he never even heard of before. *Anon.*
ADVERTISING MAN. Yessir, Nosir, Ulcer. *Lee H. Bristol*

ADVICE. A commodity more blessed to give than to receive.
— A thing sought by all, but taken by none, including the one
who gives it. *Harry Ruby*
GOOD ADVICE. What a man gives when he gets too old to
set a bad example. *La Rochefoucauld*

AESOPHAGUS. The author of Aesop's Fables. *Anon., Jr.*

AFFECTION. As different from love as day and night.
— Love by the fireside.
PASSION. Love in the flames.
LOVE. The banked fires of passion.

AFRICA. A continent short on bridges. *John Gunther*

AFTERNOON. That part of the day spent figuring how we
wasted the morning.
AFTERNOON SNACK. The pause that refleshes.
Mary B. Michael

AGE. Your length in years.
— To be seventy years young is sometimes far more cheerful
and hopeful than to be forty years old.
Dr. Oliver Wendell Holmes

AGENT. A man with a pushcart selling unlaid eggs on con-
signment after charging the hens for laying them, the
customer for buying them, and the eggs for being born.
Morton Thompson

AGGRESSION. Invading the issue.

AGITATOR. An amuck raker.

AGREEABLE PERSON. One who agrees with me.
Dr. Samuel Johnson

AGRICULTURIST. One who makes his money in town and
blows it in the country. *Elbert Hubbard*

AGROUND. When a boat makes the discovery that all water
has land under it. *Edwin Tunis*

AIDE DE CAMP. A male private secretary to a general.

AIR TRAVEL. Seeing less and less of more and more, faster and faster.

AISLE. A straight and narrow path.

ALADDIN. The original Light & Power Company.
*Don Quinn**

ALARM CLOCK. A device for awakening childless households.

ALAS. Early Victorian for "oh, hell."   *Oliver Herford*

ALASKA. Miles and miles of miles and miles.   *Anon. GI.*

ALBUM. A family rogues' gallery.

ALCOHOL. The social lubricant.   *Dr. Edward Strecker*
— An anesthetic against reality.

ALGEBRA. The wife of Euclid.   *Anon., Jr.*

ALIAS. A pen name.

ALI BABA. Being away when the crime was committed.
Anon., Jr.

ALIMONY. A system by which, when two people make a mistake, one of them keeps paying for it.   *Peggy Joyce*
— A man's cash surrender value.   *Anon.*
— The original "go now, pay later" plan.
— The high cost of leaving.   *Anon.*
— Paying an installment on a car after the wreck.
Gordon Gordon
— The wages of sin.   *Carolyn Wells*
— The divorce evil.   *Anon.*
— When a husband no longer has to bring the money home to his wife—he can mail it.   *Morty Craft*

ALLEGE. To state with fear of contradiction.

ALLEGORY. A form of literature in which virtues are made vices.   *Anon., Jr.*

ALPHABET SOUP. Loose talk, with vegetables.   *Don Quinn**

ALTAR. A place in church where a bride alters her name.
Anon., Jr.

ALTERCATION. An argument over a ready-to-wear suit.

ALTRUISM. Mowing your neighbor's lawn. *Harry Thompson*

ALUMNI. A group of college graduates who attend football games on Saturday to find reasons to fire the coach on Monday. *Jimmy Cannon*

AMAZON. A lady killer.

AMBASSADOR. An honest man, sent to lie abroad for the good of his country. *Izaak Walton*
— A man who had the most money and the fewest votes.
John D. Lodge

AMBIGUITY. Having two wives living at the same time.
Anon., Jr.

AMBITION. A poor excuse for not having sense enough to be lazy. *Charlie McCarthy*

AMBULANCE. The shuttle between a speeding automobile and a wheel chair.
— A crash & carry car.
— Something that runs in front of a shyster lawyer.
Fibber McGee

AMBUSCADE. A military ambush.

AMBUSH. A small ambuscade.

AMEN. The last word.

AMERICA. A country composed of 120,000,000 school children. *Paul Poiret, 1920*
— A country whose youth is one of her oldest and most hallowed traditions. *Oscar Wilde*
— A country that has leapt from barbarism to decadence without touching civilization. *John O'Hara*

— A nation that conceives many odd inventions for getting so ewhere but can think of nothing to do when it gets there. *Will Rogers*

— A continent discovered solely by the prophecies of Isaiah about a new heaven and a new hell. *Christopher Columbus*

— The result of an error in navigation.

AMERICAN. One who will cheerfully respond to every appeal except to move back in a bus. *Senator Soaper*

— A man who is free to choose his own form of government—blond, brunette, or redhead. *Joseph Cossman*

— A person who isn't afraid to bawl out the President, but who is always polite to a policeman.

— A sort of queer Englishman. *Agatha Christie*

— A man with two arms and four wheels. *Chinese child*

AMERICAN ENTERPRISE. Making toeless shoes a fashion instead of a calamity. *Anon.*

AMERICAN LANGUAGE. English run over by a musical comedy. *Mr. Dooley*

AMERICAN NOVEL. A story in which two people want each other from the beginning but don't get each other until the end of the book.

FRENCH NOVEL. A story in which the two people get together right at the beginning, but from then until the end of the book they don't want each other any more.

RUSSIAN NOVEL. A story in which the two people don't want each other or get each other—and for 800 pages brood about it. *Erich Maria Remarque*

AMERICAN PLAN. A scheme for shortening human life through overeating. *Elbert Hubbard*

AMERICANS. People with more time-saving devices and less time than any other people in the world.
Thomaston (Ga.) Times

— Anglo-Saxons relapsed into semibarbarism.
Bayard Taylor

— People who feel rich because they charge each other so much. *Anon.*

AMULET. A Danish omelet. *British schoolboy*

ANACHRONISM. A thing that a man puts in writing in the past before it has taken place in the future. *Anon., Jr.*

ANALOGY. The explanation of one thing by something that has no connection.

ANALYSIS. An excuse to take something to pieces to see how it works.

ANARCHIST. A baffled dictator. *Benito Mussolini*

ANATOMY. Something everyone has but it looks better on a girl. *Bruce Raeburn*
— The study of heavenly bodies. *Anon., Jr.*

ANCESTOR WORSHIP. The conviction that your family is better dead than alive.

ANCESTRY. A problem in multiplication, to which you are the answer.

ANCHOR. A ship's brake.

ANECDOTE. A joke that has seen better days.

ANGEL. A pedestrian who forgot to jump. *Ozzie Nelson*
— In heaven, nobody in particular. *G. B. Shaw*
— A five-letter word meaning a heavenly body with a long, luminous tail. *Anon., Jr.*

ANGER. A wind which blows out the lamp of the mind.
Robert Ingersoll
— Burning the candle with a blow torch.

ANGLER. A man who spends rainy days sitting around on the muddy banks of rivers doing nothing because his wife won't let him do it at home. *Irish News*

ANIMAL. An ingenious machine to which nature has given senses so that it may renew itself, and so that, up to a certain point, it may be safe from everything tending to destroy or disable itself. *Jean Jacques Rousseau*

ANIMAL HUSBANDRY. The act of having more than one husband at the same time.   *Anon., Jr.*

ANNO DOMINI. After death.   *Anon., Jr. (British Division)*

ANON. An author whose words are familiar, but whose name escapes us.
ANON., JR. A clever little bastard.
ANONYMOUS. A married author writing about women.
                    Anon.

ANT. There are two kinds; insects and lady uncles. Sometimes they live in holes and sometimes they crawl into the sugar bowl, and sometimes they live with their married sisters.   *Anon. collegiate*
ANTEATER. A picnicker.   *Anon. collegiate*

ANTARCTIC. Snowman's land.

ANTHOLOGY. A literary work written by two or three other fellows.
ANTHOLOGIST. A person who uses scissors and taste.
                    Philip Van Doren Stern
— A squirrel who thinks literature is the nuts. *Anon., Jr.*

ANTHROPOLOGY. An apology for man.

ANTIDOTE. A story a doctor tells his patients to make them feel well.   *Anon., Jr.*
— A story hastily told by the hostess to clear the air.
                    Anon., Jr.
— A funny story that you have heard before.   *Anon., Jr.*

ANTIPODES. Animals without legs, such as snakes, etc.
                    Anon., Jr.

ANTIQUE. Something that's too old to be anything but expensive.   *Denise Lor*
— Something no one would be seen with if there were more of them, but which everyone wants when no one else has any.   *Anon., Jr.*
ANTIQUE SHOPPE. A junk yard in the parlor.

ANTONYM. The opposite of the word you're trying to think of.

APARTMENT. A place where you start to turn off your TV and find you've been listening to the neighbor's.
                              The Heating Equipment Dealer

APE. An animal with the effrontery to resemble man.
— The only other animal that kisses.   *Strand Magazine*

APHRODITE. A germ which causes sickness.   *Anon., Jr.*

APOLOGIZE. To repeat an insult with variations.

APPEAL. An appeal, Hennessy, is when ye ask wan court to show its contempt for another court.   *Mr. Dooley*

APPENDICITUS. A disease caused by information in the appendix.   *Anon., Jr.*

APPENDIX. Your infernal organ.   *John Barclay, M.D.*
— A part of a book for which nobody ever found a use.
                              Anon., Jr. (British Division)

APPETIZERS. Those little bits you eat until you lose your appetite.

APPLAUSE. Palmistry for artistry.
— The generation of wind by the hands.

APRIL 1. The day we are reminded of what we are the other 364.   *Mark Twain*

ARAB. A man who will pull down a whole temple to have a stone to sit on.   *Arabian proverb*

ARCHAEOLOGY. Frozen history.   *Gregory Mason*
— Digging up the past.   *Leonard Woolley*

ARCHITECT. A fellow who talks you into debt three or four thousand dollars more.   *Abe Martin*
  ARCHITECTURE. Frozen music.   *Mme. de Staël*
  — Frozen music.   *Goethe*
  — Frozen music.   *Napoleon*
  — Frozen music.   *Alfred Austin*
  — Frozen music.   *Milton Berle*

ARGUMENT. A discussion which has two sides and no end.
                                         Leonard Neubauer*
  HEATED ARGUMENT. The ones your wife starts.

ARITHMETIC. Being able to count up to twenty without taking
  off your shoes.   *Mickey Mouse*

ARMADILLO. An ornamental shrub.   *Anon., Jr.*

ARMISTICE. A pause to permit the losing side to breed new
  soldiers.

ARMY. A body of men assembled to rectify the mistakes of
  the diplomats.   *Josephus Daniels*

ARNOLD, BENEDICT. A writer.   *Henry Ford*

AROMA. A whisper heard by the nose.

ARSONIST. A man with a burning desire.   *Ethel Meglin*
  — A person who sets the world on fire—in a small way.

ART. Taking liberties with nature.   *Melvin Lester**
  — Expensive wall paper.
  — Drawing the line somewhere.   *G. K. Chesterton*
    ART SCHOOL. A place for young girls to pass the time be-
    tween high school and marriage.   *Thomas Hart Benton*
    ARTIST. A man who won't prostitute his art, except for
    money.   *Henry Meyers**
  — An exhibitionist by profession.   *Vincent W. Van Gogh*
  — One whose career always begins tomorrow.
                                         John McN. Whistler
    ARTISTE. A foreign actress or trapeze performer.

ARTHRITIS. Twinges in the hinges.   *G. B. Howard*

ARTICHOKE. A strip tease with mayonnaise.   *Bob Hope*
  — An ancient instrument of torture.   *Anon., Jr.*

ASS. A public singer with a good voice and no ear.
                                         Ambrose Bierce
  — A public singer with good ears and no voice.
  — The masculine of lass.   *Anon., Jr. (British Division)*

ASSASSINATE. To rub out a big figure.
  ASSASSINATION. The extreme form of censorship.
  G. B. Shaw

ASTERISK. A printer's sign used to distract the reader.*

ASTROLOGY. Stars explaining man.
  ASTRONOMY. Man explaining the stars.

ASTRONAUT. A cloud-hopper.

ASYLUM. A refuge where unusual people are protected from the world.

ATHEISM. A religion in effect in fair weather.
  English proverb
  ATHEIST. A man who has no invisible means of support.
  John Buchan
  — A believer in man as the highest being.

ATHLETE. A dignified bunch of muscles unable to split wood or sift the ashes. *Indiana Bored Walk*
— (Professional) One who goes through the motions without the emotions. *College Humor*

ATLANTIC CROSSING. A cumbersome way to travel, dragging a night club and swimming pool with you. *Roy F. Layton*

ATLAS MOUNTAINS. Enormous mounds of ice cream . . . rising . . . out of an ocean of consommé. *John Gunther*

ATOM. A subdivision of matter that is likely to be the death of the subdivision business.

ATROCITY. An incident too bad to be true.

ATTIC. At once a family museum and a fireman's nightmare.
  Grace Nies Fletcher

AU REVOIR. French leave.

AUCTIONEERING. Inciting a mob for profit.

---

* Like this.

AUDIENCE. A collection of people willing to pay to be bored.

AUGUST. The month you can't open the bus window which you couldn't close in December.   *Noel Wical*

AUGUSTAN ERA. A mistake of Augustus.
                                    Anon., Jr. (British Division)

AUSTERITY. A very ancient religion but nowadays even politicians believe it.   *Anon., Jr. (British Division)*

AUTHOR. A man you can shut up by closing a book.
— A person who can read and do imitations.
— A man who lives on the royalties he expects.

AUTOBIOGRAPHY. The life of an animal written after it is dead as a moral.   *Anon., Jr. (British Division)*
— The life story of an automobile.   *Anon., Jr.*

AUTOGRAPH. A literacy test.

AUTOMAT. The first restaurant to make it possible for the poor man to enjoy food served under glass.   *Fred Allen*

AUTOMOBILE. A four-wheeled vehicle that runs up hills and down pedestrians.
— A guided missile.   *Anon.*
— Something your son manages to drive into the garage on the last drop of gas.   *Fay De Witt*
— The down payment on a finance company.
                                    *Morton Thompson**

AVENUE. A street with trees on it.
— A street that formerly had trees on it.
— A street that should have trees on it.

AVIARY. A place where birds of a different feather flock together.

AVIATION. The Elizabeth Taylor of transportation.
— Bird imitations on a commercial scale.

AVOCATION. That which one does not for a living.

AWE. Respect with the mouth wide open.

AX. Sharp medicine, but a cure for all diseases.
Sir Walter Raleigh

AXIOM. A statement that no one but George Bernard Shaw
can contradict.   *George Bernard Shaw*
— A thing that is so visible that it is not necessary to see it.
Anon., Jr.

B

B Picture. A film so bad that the kids can hardly sit through it twice.

Baby. A little rivet in the bonds of matrimony.
Arthur Gordon
— A perfect example of minority rule. *Milwaukee Journal*
— Something that gets you down in the daytime and up at night. *Kate M. Owney*
— An alimentary canal with a loud voice at one end and no responsibility at the other. *Elizabeth I. Adamson*
— A pleasant idiot.

Bachelor. A man who comes to work each morning from a different direction.
— A man who never makes the same mistake once.
Ed Wynn
— A man who never has to explain how he got the lipstick on his handkerchief.
— A man who never owned a car at college.
Fred Chiaventone
— A man who has never weakened during a weekend.
G. L. Knapp
— An average male over twenty-one whom no average female ever has made a serious attempt to marry. *H. L. Mencken*
— A goose sans water. *Russian proverb*
— A man who is dancing when he walks the floor with baby.
— A thing of beauty and a boy forever. *Helen Rowland*
— A selfish, undeserving guy who has cheated some woman out of a divorce. *Don Quinn**
— A guy linked with many girls.

Married man. A guy handcuffed to just one.
Martha Kay

— A man who can take a nap on top of the bedspread.

Anon.

BACHELOR GIRL. A girl who is still looking for a bachelor.

BACILLUS. A microbe on the make. *Frank Scully*

BACON. A hog-caller's visiting card. *Don Quinn**

BADGE. An emblem that distinguishes a delegate from a normal person. *Cynic's Cyclopaedia*
— An emblem that distinguishes a detective from an honest citizen.

BAGPIPES. The original Scotch high bawl. *Oliver Herford*

BAKED ALASKA. A sultry Good Humor.

BALCONY. A shelf for people.

BALD. Having less hair to comb but more face to wash.

Anon., Jr.

BALDNESS. Gaining face. *Earl Wilson*

BALLETOMANE. Someone who wants new ballets and free tickets. *Sol Hurok*

BAMBOO. An Italian baby. *Anon., Jr.*

BAND. An orchestra without guts.

BANK. An institution where you can borrow money if you can prove you don't need it. *Joe E. Lewis*
BANKER. A pawnbroker with a manicure. *Jackson Parks**
— A fellow who lends you his umbrella when the sun is shining and wants it back the minute it begins to rain.

Mark Twain

BANKRUPT. One who has divorced himself from debt in the hope of an early remarriage.
BANKRUPTCY. When you put your money in your pants pocket and give your coat to your creditors.

Paul Steiner

BANQUET. A $2 dinner served in sufficient numbers to enable the caterer to charge $10 for it.

BAR. A counter that separates drinkers from their money.
BARMAID. What the boys in the backroom will have.
BARTENDER. The contact man for Bacchus.   *Fred Allen*

BARBARISM. Killing a stranger and taking his wife.
CIVILIZATION. Waiting for an acquaintance to go on a trip and then taking his wife.

BARBER. A man who prostitutes his shaving.

BARGAIN. Usually something that's so reasonable they won't take it back when you find out what's wrong with it.
BARGAIN SALE. A place where a woman ruins one dress while she buys another.   *Fort Mifflin Bulletin*

BASEBALL. A game which consists of tapping a ball with a piece of wood, then running like a lunatic.   *H. J. Dutiel*
BASEBALL BROADCAST. A program that teaches children the benefits of beer swilling and cigarette smoking.
Jimmy Cannon
BASEBALL COMMISSIONER. A czar with absolute powers over anything that doesn't concern baseball.   *Jimmy Cannon*

BASEMENT DEN. A place where you can watch television when your wife isn't hanging the wash.
William V. Shannon
BASSINET. A high-class crib.

BASTARD. The end product of unplanned parenthood.
Caskie Stennett
— A hereditary title.
— The offspring of a man who has his children in his wife's name.

BASTILLE. A place of refinement for prisoners.   *Anon., Jr.*

BAT. An air-minded mouse.   *Dude's Dictionary*
BAT BOY. A middle-aged man who thought he was going to be a ballplayer when he grew up.   *Jimmy Cannon*

BATHING BEAUTY. A small-town girl with a ticket to Atlantic City.

BATHING SUIT. Two bandanas and a worried look.

Judy Canova's writers

SHOWER BATH. A leetle room that rains. *Pepito*

BATON. A thin white line that a conductor keeps drawing to underscore the score.

BAUDELAIRE. Vice versa.

BAY. A body of water surrounded by restaurants.

Joe Candullo

BEANS. Actor's caviar. *Fred Allen*

BEAST. A man being sued for divorce.

BEAUTY. The pleasure of lines, masses, sounds.
— A snare: especially to them that haven't got it.

Mrs. Whitney

— A soft, smooth, slippery thing. *Plato*

BEAUTICIAN. A panhandler. *Anon.*

BED. The only perfect climate. *Anon.*
— If bed is the perfect climate, why do so many people die there?
— A multiplication table.
— The grave of lost illusions. *Cynic's Cyclopaedia*

HOSPITAL BED. A parked taxi with the meter running.

Frank Scully

BEE. A buzzy busybody.

BEGGARS. Vermin that infest the rich. *French proverb*

BEHEADING. A little necking overdone. *Fred Allen*

BELCH. An after-dinner speech.

BENEDICTION. A curse in reverse.

BENEFACTOR. One who returns part of his loot.

BENNETT, ARNOLD. A soldier in the war on the Union side. He turned traitor to the Union, was injured in battle, and then he begged to be allowed to put on his union suit.

Anon., Jr.

BETROTH. To ring a belle.

BETTER. What every girl should know. *Charley Jones*

BEVERLY HILLS. A part of the country where the bizarre is sedate. *Jerry D. Lewis*
— The most beautiful slave quarters in the world. *Moss Hart*

BEVIN, ERNEST. A bumblebee that's gotten into a cobweb and thinks he's the spider. *The Week* (London)

BIBLE. A handbook for travelers by authors who haven't been there.

BIBLIOMANIAC. A person who reads the Bible incessantly from cover to cover. *Anon., Jr.*

BIERCE, AMBROSE. A wit who played the devil with the dictionary.

BIG-GAME HUNTING. The slaughter of animals made ferocious by the presence of hunters. *Jimmy Cannon*

BIGAMIST. A man who marries a beautiful girl and a good cook. *Chicago Herald-American*
— A lion-tamer working in two cages simultaneously.
— A man who makes the same mistake twice. *Anon.*
— A man who has two wives, of course,
    Is always called a bigamist;
But when he has some three or four,
    We guess he is a pigamist. *Florida Times Union*
— The greedy guy who gets so far
    From being a monogamist
As to have spouses five, I'd call
    A matrimonial hogamist. *E.B., Boston Transcript*
— A heavy Italian fog. *Anon.*

BIGAMY. The only crime on the books where two rites make a wrong. *Bob Hope*
— Respectability carried to criminal lengths.

Constantine FitzGibbon

— Having one wife too many.
MONOGAMY. The same thing. *Anon.*

BIGOTRY. The disease of ignorance. *Thomas Jefferson*
— An obstinate attachment to more than one wife. *Anon., Jr.*

BILIOUS. That nauseated feeling you get when you open the mail the first of the month. *Mike Connolly*

BINNACLE. The plural of monocle. *Anon., Jr.*

BIOGRAPHY. A region bounded on the north by history, on the south by fiction, on the east by obituary, and on the west by tedium. *Philip Guedalla*

BIRCH SOCIETY. The Ku Klux Klan without nightshirts.

Harry S Truman

BIRTH. The beginning of death.
  BIRTH ANNOUNCEMENT. A stork quotation.

Portsmouth *Herald*

  BIRTH CONTROL. A proposition which would be even more attractive if it could be made retroactive.

Weston *Leader*

— Copulation without population. *Anon.*

BITCH. A female of a dog or vice versa.

BLACK TIE OPTIONAL. Go ahead and be a slob if you want to.
Earl Wilson

BLACKGUARD. A man who has just ruined one's sister.

BLADDER. The human apparatus that pays the tax on beer.

BLANC MANGE. The highest peak in the Alps. *Anon., Jr.*

BLANKET. An Indian's overcoat. *Dude's Dictionary*

BLINKERS. Eye shields put on horses so they won't be frightened by getting a look at the horse players who bet on them. *Jimmy Cannon*

BLIZZARD. The inside of a fowl. *Anon., Jr.*

BLOCKHEAD. One who thinks in limited circumstances.

BLOOD. That fragile scarlet tree we carry within us.
Sir Osbert Sitwell

BLOTTER. Something you look for while the ink dries. *Anon.*

BLOTTO. Having blotted.

BLUNDERBUSS. A baby carriage. *Anon.*

BLURT. To speak the truth.

BOASTER. A person with whom it is no sooner done than said.
Milwaukee *Journal*
— Someone invited for the evening who proves that the night has a thousand I's. *Eastern Shore News*

BOB. A fake genuflex. *Anon.*

BODY. A pair of pincers set over a bellows and a stewpan, the whole fixed upon stilts. *Samuel Butler*
— An envelope. *Dr. Alexis Carrel*

BOER WAR. A pig fight put on for the pleasure of Louis XIV.
Anon., Jr.

BOHEMIAN. A gypsy in a rut.

BOLT. A thing like a stick of hard metal, such as iron, with a square bunch on one end and a lot of scratches going round and round the other end.
NUT. Similar to the bolt only just the opposite, being a hole in a little square of iron sawed off short with rings also around the inside of the hole. *Will Mackey*

BON JOUR. A fine how-do-you-do.

Bon Vivant. A man who would rather be a good liver than have one.

Boner. The other guy's mistake.   *Leonard Neubauer**

Book. A tool for sharpening the brain.
    book jacket. A fable of contents.   *Gary Belkin*
    books. The curse of the human race.   *Disraeli*
    bookie. A pickpocket who lets you use your own hands.
                                         Henry Morgan
    bookworm. An intellectual hookworm.
    rare book. A borrowed volume that comes home.   *Anon.*

Boomerang. A working model of poetic justice.
— A weapon invented by a Scotchman.
                           Pennsylvania *Punch Bowl*

Bop. The kind of music no matter what you play wrong it comes out right.   *Hal Jackson*

Bore. The kind of man who, when you ask him how he is, tells you.   *Channing Pollock*
— A person who is here today and here tomorrow.   *Anon.*
— A guy who monopolizes the conversation when you have something brilliant to say.   *Anon.*
— A person who deprives you of solitude without providing you with company.   *Gian Vincenzo Gravina*
— A person who has flat feats.   *Joe Harrington*
— The last one to find himself out.
                Dr. Oliver Wendell Holmes
— A man in love with another woman.
                Mary Pettingbone Poole
— A guy who never seems to have a previous engagement.
                Anon.
    boredom. Rent for living in this world.   *Bill Manville*
    — The anteroom of Hell.

Borrowers (Book). Mutilators of collections, spoilers of the symmetry of shelves, and creators of odd volumes.
                Charles Lamb

BORSCHT. Beet soup with high blood pressure.
                                                      *Sam Pokrass**

BOSS. The man at the office who is early when you're late and
    late when you're early.   *Take It or Leave It*

BOSWELL, JAMES. A scholar and a Christian and a brute.
                                                      Soame Jenyns

BOTANIST. A man who knows all about flowers.
    FLO IST. A man who knows how much people will pay for
        them.   Lebanon, Kan., *Times*
    BOTANY. The art of insulting flowers in Greek and Latin.
                                                      Alphonse Karr

BOUDOIR. Room for improvement.

BOULEVARD. An expensive street.

BOUNDER. One who crosses the wrong boundaries.

Bow. A fiddlestick.

BOWERY. A shady thoroughfare in New York City.

BOWLING. Marbles for grown-ups.

BOXING. Tap dancing with gloves on.
    BOXING COMMISSION. A punch board.   *Don Quinn**
    BOXING COMMISSIONER. A public official who sits in the first
        row at fights and denounces wrestling.   *Jimmy Cannon*

BOY. The appetite of a horse, the digestion of a sword swal-
    lower . . . the curiosity of a cat, the lungs of a dictator, the
    imagination of a Paul Bunyan, the shyness of a violet, the
    audacity of a steel trap, the enthusiasm of a firecracker,
    and when he makes something he has five thumbs on each
    hand.   *Alan Beck*
— Of all the wild beasts, the most difficult to manage. *Plato*
— A noise with dirt on it.   *Punch*
    BOY SCOUT. A boy who washes behind the ears one night
        a week.
    — A friend to all and a bother to every other scout.
                                                      Anon., Jr.

BOYHOOD. A summer sun. *Edgar Allan Poe*
BOYS. Unwholesome companions for grown people.
Charles Lamb

BOYCOTT. A conspiracy not to obey that impulse.

BRAIN. That with which we think we think.
BRAINS. What you-all just *got* to use when you ain't got an
education. *Eliza*

BRAND. A horse's monogram. *Dude's Dictionary*

BRANDY HANGOVER. The wrath of grapes.

BRASSIERE. A bust stop. *Bob Levinson**
— A device to bring out a girl's best points.

BRAT. A cherub that slipped.

BRAWL. A kind of dance. *Shakespeare*

BRAZIER. The kind of garment the Italians wore instead of
having their houses heated by furnaces. *Anon., Jr.*

BREAKFAST (Kentucky). A big beefsteak, a quart of bourbon,
and a hound dog. The dog is there to eat the beefsteak.
Frederick Philip Stieff
BREAKFAST IN BED. The hardest meal for a mother to get.

BREAST. Child's restaurant.
— The fountain of youth.

BREATH. The material from which voice is made.
Olive Day Monat

BREEDING. Concealing how much we think of ourselves and
how little we think of the other person. *Mark Twain*
GOOD BREEDING. An expedient to make fools and wise men
equals. *Richard Steele*

BREVITY. The next best thing to silence. *Anon.*
— The soul of lingerie. *Dorothy Parker*

BRIBERY. Using money as a blindfold.
— Paying Paul to rob Peter.

BRIDE. A goddess who does the dishes.
    BRIDEGROOM. He for whom the bride is groomed.

BRIDGE. An unfriendly game of cards.   *Troy Times*
— The triumph of mind over chatter.
                                  Four Hundred & Four

BRITISH. Germans pretending to be French.   *Max Eastman*
    BRITISH EMPIRE. A domain created in a moment of world
    absent-mindedness.   *Eamon de Valera*

BROADCLOTH. The kind used for Jackie Gleason's pants.
                                      Nat Pendleton

BROAD-MINDEDNESS. The result of flattening high-mindedness
    out.   *George Saintsbury*

BROADWAY. A place where people spend money they haven't
    earned to buy things they don't need to impress people
    they don't like.   *Walter Winchell*
— America's hardened artery.   *Mark Kelly*
— A street of ham and aches.   *Hy Gardner*
    BROADWAYITE. One who hasn't the carfare to Hollywood.
                                  Gypsy Rose Lee

BROCHURE. A handbill with kid gloves.

BROKER. A man who runs your fortune into a shoestring.
                              Alexander Woollcott

BRONTË. One of three English novelists . . . but especially
    Charlotte.   *Funk & Wagnalls' Desk Standard Dictionary*

BROOKLYN. The left bank of the East River.   *Le Corbusier*

BROWN DERBY RESTAURANT. The place where tourists mistake
    one another for film stars.   *Fred Allen*

BRUIN. The art of making beer.   *Anon., Jr.*

BUDGET. A schedule for going into debt systematically.

— Telling your money where to go instead of wondering where it went. *C. E. Hoover*

— A method of worrying before you spend money, as well as afterward. *Dorothy Malone's press agent*

BUFFALO BILL. An important bill passed in 1854. *Anon., Jr.*

BUFFET DINNER. Where the hostess doesn't have enough chairs for everybody. *Earl Wilson*

BUFFOON. A sheep in clown's clothing.

BUG. A domesticated insect.

BULLDOZER. A sergeant's chin with a motor in it.
Bob Hope's writers

BULLET. Son of a gun. *Siamese student*

BUN. The lowest form of wheat. *Michigan Gargoyle*

BUNCO. The dissemination of knowledge in the rural districts.
Foolish Dictionary

BUREAUCRACY. The people who put in their place the people who put them in their places.

BUREAU OF IMMIGRATION. The agency that prevents it.
Leo C. Rosten

BURIAL. Being put to bed with a shovel.

BURLESQUE. A take-off.

— Actually, *burleque*, an old Latin expression meaning "Bring on the broads." *Red Buttons*

BURP. A belch under wraps. *Leonard Neubauer*°

BURR. A hitch-hiking seed.

BUSINESS. The art of extracting money from another man's pocket without resorting to violence. *Max Amsterdam*

— Capitalized cannibalism.

— What, when you don't have any, you go out of.   *Anon.*
BIG BUSINESS. A polite form of larceny, founded on the
  faith of the stockholders that they, too, will get theirs.

BUST. Something a lady wears.   *Anon., Jr.*

BUSTLE. A fender on a bender.
— An annex in the rear with decorative intent.
— A cushion for the sitting room.
— A false front in the rear.
— A deceitful seatful.   *Anon.*

BUSYBODY. A person with an interferiority complex.
                                        Calgary *Herald*
BUTCHER. A swindler on a small scale.

BUTLER, SAMUEL. The President of Columbia College. He
  wrote *The Way of All Fish*.   *Anon., Jr.*

BUTTOCK. A cushion for the sitting room.

BUTTRESS. A woman who makes butter.   *Anon., Jr.*

C

CABBAGE. A familiar kitchen-garden vegetable about as large and wise as a man's head. *Ambrose Bierce*

CACKLE. The commercial announcement of a hen.

CAD. A term formerly applied to a man who would try to take advantage of a young girl's innocence. He is now called an optimist. *Ted Cook*
— A man who doesn't know how to insult a lady.
— An old caddie. *Russell Patterson**
    CADDIE. A small cad.
    — A boy employed at a liberal stipend to lose balls for others and to find them for himself.

                        Foolish Dictionary, 1904
    — A golfing expert who loses balls for you in one round, so that he can find them for himself in the next.

                       Cynic's Cyclopaedia, 1926

CAFÉ SOCIETY. The international white trash. *Vincent Price*

CAFETERIA. An eating place designed on the principle that the customer's eyes are bigger than his stomach.

CALENDAR. An attempt, underwritten by the principal religions, to make the heavenly bodies keep regular hours.

CALIFORNIA. A state that's washed by the Pacific on one side and cleaned by Las Vegas on the other. *Al Cooper*
— A fine place to live—if you happen to be an orange.
                           Fred Allen
    CALIFORNIA SMOG. It's like God had squeezed a big onion over Los Angeles. *Jack Paar*

36

CALLIOPE. A steam-heated musical instrument.
Cynic's Cyclopaedia

CALVES. One of the by-products of cattle-raising.   *Anon., Jr.*

CAMARADERIE. The affection shown by one chorus boy for another on stage.

CAMEL. An animal that ruined its shape trying to get through the eye of a needle.
— A horse with knobs.   *Peter Duke*
— A warped horse.   *Mutt & Jeff*
— An animal that looks as though it had been put together by a committee.   *Anon.*
   CAMELOPARD. An Abyssinian animal, taller than an elephant, but not so thick; so named because he has a neck and head like a camel, is spotted like a pard; but his spots are white upon a red ground. The Italians call him *giaraffa*.   *Dr. Samuel Johnson*

CAMERA. A crank with a glass eye.   *Glen N. Wilkinson°*

CAN. A piece of tin that costs the housewife more than the food it's wrapped around.   *Consumer's Union*

CANAL. A long straight ditch, filled with water, and drawn by a mule.   *Anon., Jr.*

CANDIDATE. A person who gets money from the rich and votes from the poor to protect them from each other.
                                                             Anon.
— A politician who stands for what he thinks people will fall for.   *Anon.*

CANDY. Candy is dandy
         But liquor
         Is quicker.   *Ogden Nash*
— A good food, pure and wholesome. It is a universal food; it speaks all languages; it dries the tears in the eyes of little children; it wreathes the faces of old age in smiles; it brings joy to the home; it is the advance agent of happiness in every clime.   *National Confectioners Association*

CANNIBAL. A guy who goes into a restaurant and orders the
waiter.   *Jack Benny*
— One who really loves his fellow man.

CANNON. The last reason of kings.   *Anon. Frenchman*

CAP. A bean bag.   *College Humor*

CAPITALISM. The theory that the biggest pea owns the pod.
— The belief that heaven will protect the working girl.
  CAPITALIST. One who will do almost anything for the poor
  except get off their backs.   *Tolstoy*

CAPRICE. A fancy fancy.

CAR. A misguided missile.   *Anon.*
  CAR SICKNESS. The feeling you get each month when the
  payment is due.

CARAMEL. A substance for extracting children's teeth.

CAREER. A job that starts after 10 A.M.   *Frank Jones*

CARICATURE. The tribute that mediocrity pays to genius.
                                                      Oscar Wilde

CARPENTER. A man who hits the nail on the head for a living.

CARTE BLANCHE. Take Blanche home.   *Arthur Godfrey*

CARTEL. An international money belt.

CARUSO, ROBINSON. A great singer who lived on an island.
                                                       Anon., Jr.

CASANOVA. A ladybug.

CASTING (Hollywood). Deciding which of two faces the
public is least tired of.

CAT. A quadruped, the legs, as usual, being at the four
corners.   *Anon., Jr.*
— An example of sophistication without civilization.
— A housebroken panther.
— A creature that plays with mice and pretends they're men.

— A lady cad.
— A pygmy lion who loves mice, hates dogs, and patronizes human beings. *Oliver Herford*

CATACOMBS. Where the early Christians lived when they were put to death by Nero. *Anon., Jr.*

CATALOGUE. A dialogue by kitties. *Anon., Jr.*

CATASTROPHE. A broken fingernail in eternity.

CATCH. To succeed in one's pursuit.
— To catch a train—missing the train before.
G. K. Chesterton

CATCHUP. A disguise for steaks.

CATERPILLAR. An upholstered worm. *Mickey Mouse*

CATHARSIS. A psychological means of stopping a catarrh. It illustrates the influence of mind over body. *Anon., Jr.*

CATHERINE THE GREAT. A vulture for culture.

CAUCUS. A dead animal. *Anon., Jr.*

CAULIFLOWER. A cabbage with a college education.
Mark Twain

CAVALCADE. A parade in which the horses furnish the dignity.

CAVE CANEM. Beware! I may sing! *Anon., Jr.*

CAVIAR. The eggs of a surgeon. *Anon., Jr.*

CAW. A crow's crow.

CELIBACY. A unit of land in the Mohammedan system.
Anon., Jr.
— A disease of the brain. *Anon., Jr.*
   CELIBATE. An old refrain.

CELEBRITY. The advantage of being known to people who don't know you. *Chamfort*

— A man who owns his own tuxedo.   *Ted Strong*
— A nonentity who has been on television twice.   *Vic Perry*

CELERY. A vegetable which should be seen and not heard.

CEMETERY. A thickening of the plots.   *Leonard Neubauer**
— The last resort.

CENSOR. A guy who sticks his No's into other people's busi-
    ness.   *Our Army*
    CENSORSHIP. The power of the suppress.
— The clean sweep of a dirty mind.   *Don Quinn**

CENSURE. The tax a man pays to the public for being eminent.
                                          Jonathan Swift

CENSUS TAKER. A man who goes from house to house increas-
    ing the population.   *Anon., Jr.*

CENTAUR. A horse whose neck is a man.

CENTIMETER. An insect with a hundred legs.
                          Anon., Jr. (British Division)

CEREMONY. The invention of wise men to keep fools at a
    distance.   *Richard Steele*

CHAIR. Headquarters for the hindquarters.

CHAMBERLAIN, NEVILLE. The first prime minister in the his-
    tory of Great Britain to crawl on his hands and knees at
    the rate of 200 miles an hour.   *Dorothy Thompson*

CHAMOIS. A fleet-footed animal used for washing windows
    in the mountains of South America.   *Anon., Jr.*

CHAMPAGNE. The wine of least resistance. *Kenneth Taylor**
— A drink that makes you see double and feel single.

CHANTEUSE. A thirty-five-year-old Frenchwoman.
                                          Mike Wayne

CHAPERONE. One who is too old to get into the game, but still tries to intercept the passes. *Tennessee Ernie Ford*

CHAPLAIN. The rabbi who goes with the army to see that the killing is kosher.

CHARACTER. Property. *Samuel Smiles*
— Made by what you stand for; reputation, by what you fall for. *Robert Quillen*
— What you have and what the other guy is. *Joe Godman*

CHARITY. The sterilized milk of human kindness.
Oliver Herford
— Bestowing on a poor man something he could otherwise fish from your rubbish can.

CHARLATAN. Medical term for a competitor.

CHARLESTON. The place where the Ashley and Cooper rivers meet to form the Atlantic Ocean. *Anon. Charlestonian*

CHARM. Money in the bank. *Josephine Dillon Gable*

CHASE. Drama.
COMEDY: Two chasing one.
ROMANCE: One chasing one.
TRAGEDY: One chasing two.

CHASM. A nasty void.

CHASTE. She whom no one has asked. *Ovid*
— As the kiss of billiard balls. *Alex Osborn*
CHASTITY. Perhaps the most peculiar of all sexual aberrations. *Remy de Gourmont*

CHÂTEAU. Any French house in the country which isn't an out-and-out bungalow. (The bungalows they refer to as villas.) *Ilka Chase*

CHAUFFEUR. A man who is smart enough to operate an automobile, but clever enough not to own one.
Foolish Dictionary

CHAUTAUQUA. Pious vaudeville.   *Variety*

CHEAP DATE. A guy who walks you to a drive-in.
                                          Anon. Chorus Girl

CHECKBOOK. The one book that really tells you where you
    can go on your vacation.   *Imogene Fey*
    CHECKING ACCOUNT. A shrinking fund. *Leonard Neubauer*°

CHECKROOM. A place where the sheep are separated from
    the coats.

CHEESE. Milk's leap toward immortality.   *Clifton Fadiman*
— Butter gone bad.   *Anon., Jr. (British Division)*

CHEF. An interior decorator.

CHEMISE. A girl's first slip.

CHESTERFIELD. A piece of furniture made to hold three people
    with an arm at each end.   *Anon., Jr.*

CHEWING GUM. The national anthem without words.
— A dentiferous treadmill.   *Thomas A. Edison*
— A confection that gratifies the palate and cheats the
    stomach.

CHIC. Adjective for "anything with a hat to match." *Macy's*

CHICAGO. The Winded City.   *William G. Shepherd*
— A double Newark.   *Heywood Broun*

CHICKEN. The most important bird in the world.   *Beebe*
— An egg factory.   *Anon.*
— A vegetable that breaks through the hedges. *Chinese saying*

CHILD. An innocent by-product.   *Anon.*
— Someone who stands halfway between an adult and a
    TV set.   *Anon.*
— A token of affection.
    CHILD ACTOR. An example of Nature abhorring a very small
        vacuum.   *Morton Thompson*
    CHILDBIRTH. The labor of love.

CHILDREN. Why's guys. *Anon.*
— Natural mimics who act like their parents in spite of every effort to teach them good manners. *Anon.*
— Little bonds who hold a marriage together by keeping their parents too busy to quarrel with each other. *Anon.*

CHIN, RECEDING. A facial asset useful in eating corn on the cob.

CHINAMAN. A dirty heathen who robs white men of jobs they wouldn't soil their hands with.
San Francisco Hooligan, 1850s

CHISELER. A compleat angler. *Anon.*

CHIT CHAT. Chat among chits.

CHIVALRY. Opening the door and standing aside so some dame can rush in and take the job you're after.
— Going about releasing beautiful maidens from other men's castles, and taking them to your own castle.
Henry W. Nevinson
— The attitude of a man towards a strange woman.
Anon., Jr.
— The act of a man who gives his seat to a lady in a public convenience. *Anon., Jr.*
— What you feel when you're cold. *Anon., Jr.*

CHOREOGRAPHER. A lame dancer.

CHORINE. A girl who thinks that the most sinful way to get a mink coat is to pay for it herself. *David Wayne*

CHORTLE. Lewis Carroll's telescoping of "chuckle" and "snort."

CHRIST. A man who was born 5,000 years ahead of his time.
CHRISTIAN SCIENCE. When they cure you and you ain't there by thinking good things about you even if there ain't any. *Anon., Jr.*
CHRISTMAS. The time when the year comes to a head.
Anon.

CHRISTMAS JEWELRY. The first thing to turn green in the spring.   *Kin Hubbard*

CHRYSANTHEMUM. A flower in need of a haircut.

CHUMP. A champ, ten seconds later.

CHURCH. A place in which gentlemen who have never been to heaven brag about it to persons who will never get there.   *H. L. Mencken*
— Man's effort to keep a roof over God's head.
   CHURCH COLLECTION. Hush money.
   CHURCH SOCIAL. Ennui, Christian soldiers.

CIGARETTE. A fire at one end, a fool at the other, and a bit of tobacco between.   *Anon.*

CINDERELLA. A girl with little feet who had a big time.

CINEMA. A pastime for slaves.   *Georges Duhamel*
— A refuge for those who are weary of life.

CIRCLE. A line of no depth running around a dot forever.
                                        Anon., Jr.
— A round straight line with a hole in the middle. *Anon., Jr.*
— A line which meets its other end without ending.
                                        Anon., Jr.
— A round line with no kinks in it, joined up so as not to show where it began.   *Anon., Jr. (British Division)*

CIRCUMSTANTIAL EVIDENCE. Like a blackberry, which when red or white is green.   *Austin O'Malley*

CIRCUS. Animals acting like people and people acting like monkeys.

CITY. A stone forest.   *J. B. Priestley*
— A large community where people are lonesome together.
                                        Herbert V. Prochnow

CIVIL SERVICE. What you get in restaurants between wars.
                                        Harry Blackstone

CIVIL WAR. What happened when Lincoln signed the Emasculation Proclamation. *Anon., Jr.*

CIVILIZATION. An unnatural way of living.
— The rearrangement of prejudices.
— The time when men learn to live off each other instead of off the land. *Mort Sahl*
— The slow process of gradually falling in line with the visionary ideas of minorities. *Nuggets*
— The difference between a war whoop and a college yell.
— A process of making life more valuable and less precious.
— The white man's burden.
— The creation of a sewerage problem.
  CIVILIZE. To give natives a sense of shame.

CLAQUE. Hired hands. *Frank Jones*

CLARINET. An instrument that is midway between an oboe and a strait jacket. *Richard English*

CLASSIC. A good book neglected by too much appreciation.
— Something that everybody wants to have read and nobody wants to read. *Mark Twain*

CLASSMATE. A person over whose shoulder you've studied.

CLEANLINESS. Almost as bad as godliness. *Samuel Butler*

CLERGYMEN. Attorneys-at-God.

CLIMATE. What brings people to California; weather is what washes them away. *Robert Whitehead*
— What lasts all the time; weather only lasts a few days. The climate of Bombay is such that its inhabitants have to live elsewhere. *Anon., Jr.*

CLOCK. Time on tick.

CLOTHES. Wrappings worn by men for warmth, women for spite, and children because they have to.
— The coverings of sin. *Adam*

CLOUDS. The bladders of heaven.

CLOVERLEAF. A crossroads puzzle. *M. M. McKeachie, Jr.*

CLOWN. A man who acts too natural.

CLUB. The rich man's saloon.

COACH. A fellow who is always willing to lay down your life for his job. *Texas Longhorn*

COAGULATION. The only proof that blood is thicker than water.

COAL. An animal that used to be a vegetable and is now a mineral.

COCKTAIL LOUNGE. A half-lit room full of half-lit people.
Robert Q. Lewis
COCKTAIL PARTY. An affair where you meet old, old friends you never saw before. *Fulton Bryan*
— Where they serve yesterday's leftovers and tomorrow's hangovers. *Fred Chiaventone*
— A gathering held to enable forty people to talk about themselves at the same time. The man who remains after the liquor is gone is the host. *Fred Allen*

CODE OF THE WEST. Shoot first, apologize later.

COED. A girl who didn't get her man in high school.
Aunt Emma

COFFEE. The morning transfusion. *Anon.*
BLACK COFFEE. The best cure for a hangover the night before instead of the morning after. *Freeman Chum*

COGNAC. A noun I never yet declined. *Lord Byron*

COIFFURE. A French word meaning "you'll keep coming to us because you'll never be able to do it this way yourself."
Molly McGee
COIN. A round, hard, elusive object.

COINCIDE. What you do when it starts raining. *Anon., Jr.*

COINED. Humane, i.e., "He was always coined to animals."
Charlestonese

Cold. Both positive and negative. Sometimes the eyes have it and sometimes the nose. *William Lyon Phelps*
— An ailment cured in two weeks with a doctor's care, and in fourteen days without it. *C. C. Furnas*

Coleridge, Samuel. An archangel, a little damaged.
Charles Lamb

Collaboration. A literary partnership based on the false assumption that the other fellow can spell.

College. A washing machine; you get out of it just what you put in, but you'd never recognize it. *Anon. professor*
— A place where one spends several thousand dollars on an education, then prays for a holiday to come on a school day. Boston *Beanpot*
— A place to keep warm between high school and an early marriage. *George Gobel*

    college education. Something that shows a man how little other people know. *T. C. Haliburton*

    college football. A game which would be much more interesting if the faculty played instead of the students, and even more interesting if the trustees played. There would be a great increase in broken arms, legs, and necks, and simultaneously an appreciable diminution in the loss to humanity. *H. L. Mencken*

Collision. An attempt on the part of two vehicles to occupy the same space at the same time.

Colonel. A male resident of Kentucky. *Foolish Dictionary*

Colony. An outhouse of civilization.

Colorado. A state with a nine-month winter and three months of late fall. *Anon.*

Coloratura. A soprano whose voice can bounce.

Columbus. A great navigator who cursed about the Atlantic.
Anon., Jr.

COLUMNIST. A guy who finds out things that people do not
want known, and tells them to people to whom it doesn't
make any difference.   *Walter Winchell*
— A paragrafter.   *David Rose*
— A street cleaner who works with a pencil.

COMBUSTION. When two elements get together and throw
things off.   *Anon. collegian*

COMEDIAN. A guy with a good memory who hopes no one
else has.   *Red Skelton*
    MUSICAL COMEDY. Disorderly conduct occasionally inter-
    rupted by talk.   *George Ade*

COMET. A fugitive from a solar system.

COMIC STRIP. A burlesque artist who tells funny stories as
she disrobes.   *Anon., Jr.*

COMMA. What a medium falls into.   *Anon., Jr.*

COMMEMORATE. To remember with oratory.

COMMERCIAL (TV). The pause that depresses.   *Anon.*

COMMITTEE. A group that keeps minutes and wastes hours.
                                        The Traveler

COMMON SENSE. Not so common.   *Voltaire*

COMMUNIQUÉ. A rumor with epaulets.   *Arthur "Bugs" Baer*

COMMUNISM. Leftward ho!   *V. F. Calverton*
— The opiate of the asses.   *Arthur C. von Stein*
— The exploitation of the strong by the weak.
                                        Pierre Joseph Proudhon
— An impractical joke.
— Nobody's got nothin', but everybody's workin'.
                                        Fred Allen
— If you have two cows, you give them to the government
and the government gives you some milk.

DICTATORSHIP. If you have two cows, the government shoots you and keeps the cows.

CAPITALISM. If you have two cows, you sell one and buy a bull. *Supervision*

COMMUNIST. Either a republican or a monarchist who votes for the one opposite to the one he is. *Anon., Jr.*

— A socialist in a helluva hurry. *Rotary speaker*

— A fellow who borrows your pot to cook your goose in. *Hill Folks*

— A man who disagrees with the editor.

— (Rare) A member of the Communist Party.

COMMUNISTS. Smug fanatics. *Bella Spewack*

COMMUNITY CHEST. An organization that puts all its begs in one ask-it. *Reader's Digest*

COMMUTER. One who spends his life
     In riding to and from his wife;
     A man who shaves and takes a train
     And then rides back to shave again.
E. B. White

COMPATRIOT. One who has fled from the same country you have.

— A person you wouldn't speak to in the old country.

COMPLAINT. A grief résumé.

COMPLIMENT. When you say something to another which he and we know is not true. *Anon., Jr.*

— The applause that refreshes. *John W. Wierlein*

COMPOSER. A bad pianist with a good memory.

COMPROMISE. An out to stay in. *Robertson White**

— Any decision by two or more persons.

— The art of slicing a piece of cake in such a way that everyone believes he received the biggest piece. *Jan Peerce*

CONCEIT. God's gift to little men. *Bruce Barton*

CONCUBINE. The state flower of Colorado. *Anon., Jr.*

CONES. Ice cream you can walk with. *Adrian Anderson*

CONFERENCE. A meeting to decide when the next meeting will be held. *Henry Ginsberg*
— A meeting of a group of men who singly can do nothing, but who collectively agree that nothing can be done. *Fred Allen*
— A coffee break with real napkins.

CONFESSION. A voluntary admission obtained with a rubber hose.

CONFIDENCE MAN. One who lives off the fatheads of the land. *Fibber McGee*

CONFLAGRATION. A reporter's first fire.

CONFORMIST. Anyone who does not take exception to the same things you do. *Russell Baker*

CONGRESS. Bingo with billions. *Red Skelton*
— The generation of wind by the winded generation.
— A body of men brought together to slow down the government.
— A man gets up to speak, says nothing, nobody listens— and then everybody disagrees. *Russian visitor*
CONGRESSMAN. A man who represents himself in Congress.
  — A $3,000-a-year man striving desperately to hang on to a $22,500-a-year job. *Clinton Gilbert*
  — A man who votes for all appropriations and against all taxes. *Ex-Senator Henry Ashurst*

CONJUNCTION. A place where two railway lines meet. *Anon., Jr. (British Division)*

CONNUBIAL BLISS. A dream from which a man wakes to find he's married.

CONSCIENCE. A fear of being found out. *Harry Ruby*
— A trait that gets a lot of credit that belongs to cold feet.
— An inner voice that warns us somebody is looking. *H. L. Mencken*

— The still small voice that makes you feel still smaller.
James A. Sanaker

— The thing that hurts when everything else feels so good.
Anon.

NEW ENGLAND CONSCIENCE. It doesn't keep you from doing anything—but it won't let you enjoy it.

CONSERVATIVE. A man who will not look at the new moon out of respect for that ancient institution, the old one.
Douglas Jerrold

— A man who is too cowardly to fight and too fat to run.
Elbert Hubbard

— A man with two perfectly good legs who has never learned to walk.   *Franklin D. Roosevelt*

— A kind of greenhouse where you look at the moon.
Anon., Jr.

— A fellow that's in office and wants to stay there.
Huey P. Long

— One who admires radicals a century after they're dead.
Leo C. Rosten

— A man who believes nothing should be done for the first time.   *Alfred E. Wiggam*

— One who has something to conserve.

CONSONANT. A large piece of land surrounded by water.
Anon., Jr. (British Division)

CONSTITUTION. The health of a nation.

CONSULTATION. A medical court to absolve grave errors.

CONSUMER. One who believes advertisements.
    CONSUMER (ultimate). One who can't get his money back.

CONTEMPT. Dignity as a substitute for wit.

CONTENTMENT. Being satisfied with what you haven't got.
— The smother of invention.   *Ethel Watts Mumford*

CONTINENCE. The difference between prophet and lust.

CONTINENTAL KITCHEN. A real-estate term meaning: "Needs a new oven." *William V. Shannon*

CONTORTIONIST. A lady who recites pieces. *Anon., Jr.*

CONTOUR. The outline of a funny shape, such as a broken coastline or a woman. *Anon., Jr. (British Division)*

CONTRACT. An agreement to do something if nothing happens to prevent it.

CONTRALTO. A low sort of music that only ladies sing.
Anon., Jr.

CONVALESCENT. A patient who is still alive. *Dr. Leo Michel*

CONVENTION. A gathering where conventions are forgotten.

CONVERSATION. Anecdote, tempered by interruption.
Raymond Mortimer
— A vocal competition in which the one who is catching his breath is called the listener.
— The feminine of silence. *Roland Alix*
— The process of turning steam into water again. *Anon., Jr.*

COOKING. A process of preparing food which would be speeded up fifty years by the use of zippers on canned goods. *Russel Crouse*

COOLIDGE, CALVIN. The greatest man who ever came out of Plymouth Corner, Vermont. *Clarence Darrow*
— The baffling mystery of zero. *Philip Wylie*

COORDINATOR. One who can bring organized chaos out of regimented confusion. *Louis Prima*
— The man with the desk between two expediters.

COQUETTE. A loose virgin.

CORESPONDENT (Male). The right kind of man in the wrong place. *Cynic's Cyclopaedia*
— (Female). A hot-water bag.

CORNERSTONE. A piece of masonry laid by a Mason.

CORONER. A man who crowns the King.
Anon., Jr. (British Division)

CORPORATION. An artificial person that can do everything but make love.

CORPS. A dead gentleman. *Anon., Jr.*

CORPSE. A dead lady. *Anon., Jr.*
— A breathless person.

CORPULENCE. The gross total. *Cynic's Cyclopaedia*

CORRESPONDENT. A reporter with his feet on a telegraph desk.

CORROBORATE. To yes a liar.

CORRUPTION. The low use of high office.
— An evil that grows respectable with age. *Voltaire*

CORTEGE. What you buy for your girl when you take her to a dance. *Anon., Jr.*

COSIGNER. A fall guy with a fountain pen. *Anon.*

COSMOPOLITE. One who is polite to every country except your own. *Thomas Hood*

COST-OF-LIVING INDEX. A list of numbers which prove that high prices are not expensive. *Richard M. Weiss*

COSTUME. What clothing becomes when fashions change.

COUNSEL. Advice with a price tag.

COUNTERIRRITANT. A woman who shops all day and doesn't buy anything. *Wilcox Antenna*

COUNTRY. A damp sort of place where all sorts of birds fly about uncooked. *London clubman*

COURAGE. Ignorance of the facts.

COURT. A place where they dispense with justice.

Arthur Train

— (Royal). An assembly of noble and distinguished beggars.

Talleyrand

COURTROOM. The theatre of unhappiness.

COURTESY. The art of concealing natural impulses.

COURTIER. A stooge in a palace.

COURTSHIP. The period during which the girl decides whether or not she can do any better.   *Pup*

— A snappy introduction to a tedious book.   *Wilson Mizner*

COW. A domestic animal all covered with leather. Her tail, which hangs at the end, has a brush in order to shoo off flies, or else they would fall in the milk. The head is in front, and has horns growing on each side and allows room for the mouth. The horns are used for fighting and the mouth to roar with. When the food is good, she gives good milk, but when it thunders, she goes sour. *Anon., Jr.*

— An animal having four legs, two horns and a tail. It has skin all over the outside which is covered with hair. It has skin all over the inside which is called tripe. *Anon., Jr.*

— Nothing but a machine that makes grass fit for us people to eat.   *John McNulty*

— An animal very like a bull, but a bull hurts more. *Anon., Jr.*

COWARD. One who, in a perilous emergency, thinks with his legs.   *Ambrose Bierce*

COWARDICE. The surest protection against temptation.

Mark Twain

COWBOY. A bar-fly on a horse.   *Jimmy Cannon*

CRACKER. The last resort of an anchovy.

CRANBERRIES. Grapes with high blood pressure.

Robert Benchley

CRAVAT. A $3 necktie.   *Cynic's Cyclopaedia, 1926*

— A necktie that sells for $12.50 (today).

CRAZE. The other guy's hobby. *Cynic's Cyclopaedia*

CREDITORS. The people who come because the customers didn't. *Anon.*

CRÊPES SUZETTES. Four-alarm pancakes.

CRIMINAL. A person with predatory instincts who has not sufficient capital to form a corporation. *Howard Scott*
— He who gets caught.

CRISIS. The peacetime relationship between two nations.

CRITIC. Cynic. *Shakespeare*
— A eunuch—he knows what to do but can't do it. *Esquire*
— A man who pans for gold.
— A legless man who teaches running. *Channing Pollock*
— A man who expects miracles. *James Huneker*
— A fellow who despises you because you haven't got his talent. *Nunnally Johnson*
  DRAMA CRITIC. A newspaperman whose gal ran away with an actor. *Walter Winchell*
  MUSIC CRITIC. A disappointed musician.
  *Werner Richard Heymann**
  CRITICISM. Yawning as a profession.
  — A profession by which men grow important and formidable at very small expense. *Dr. Samuel Johnson*
  — What you get when you already have everything else.
  Jackie Barnett

CROONER. A singer with his heart in his throat.
— A singer with ham in his mouth. *Francis Lederer**
— A fellow who uses his mouth to sing through his nose.
  Groucho Marx

CROQUET. Chess with sweat. *Joe Laurie, Jr.*
— The polo of senility. *Jimmy Cannon*

CROQUETTE. Hash that has come to a head. *Irvin S. Cobb*

CROWD. Two women. *Turkish proverb*

CRUELTY. The brother of fear.

CRULLER. A doughnut gone crazy.   Denver *Parrakeet*

CRYING. The refuge of plain women, but the ruin of pretty ones.   *Oscar Wilde*

CUBA. An island about the size of Pennsylvania with a population of some four million politicians.   *J. P. McEvoy*

CUCKOLD. A bird that finds another egg in his nest.

CUCKOO. A bird what lays other birds' eggs in its own nest, and viva voce.   *Anon., Jr. (British Division)*

CULTURE. Keeping up six conversations when there are twelve in the room.   *Ernest Dimmnet*
— The cultivation of cults.

CUNNING. A characteristic of animals which is called discretion in men.   *La Fontaine*

CUPID. The myth of the unborn child shopping for parents.

CURIOSITY. An overpowering instinct of cats, kids, women, scientists, and other animals.

CURVE. The loveliest distance between two points. *Mae West*

CUSHION. The lap of luxury.

CYANIDE. A chemical so poisonous that one drop of it on a dog's tongue will kill the strongest man.   *Anon., Jr.*

CYCLORAMA. A painting by a scenic artist on a merry-go-round.

CYNIC. One who looks through rose-colored glasses with a jaundiced eye.
— A man who, when he smells flowers, looks around for a coffin.   *H. L. Mencken*
    CYNICISM. A euphemism for realism. Seeing things as they really are, instead of the way we'd like them to be.
        Harry Ruby

D

D.A.R. A lady with red, white, and blue corpuscles.

DACHSHUND. A little dog half-a-dog high and a dog-and-a-half long.   *Mary Ellen Herbert*
— A Great Dane after taxes.

DAFT. Not deft.

DAIRYMAID. A girl who ought to know butter.

DAMNATION. Out of the frying pan into the fire.

DANCER. One who makes motions for a living.
   DANCING. Wonderful training for girls. It's the first way they learn to guess what a man is going to do before he does it.   *Christopher Morley*
   — The only way an author can exercise publicly with a beautiful girl in his arms, and not be talked about.
                                                   Robert Fontaine

DANIEL. The founder of the Lions Club.   Colgate *Banter*

DANSEUSE. The dancer whose husband manages the troupe.

DANTE. A Methodist parson in Bedlam.   *Horace Walpole*

DAPPER. The Broadway version of debonair.

DAREDEVIL. One who rocks a boat for a living.

DATE. A sweet meet.
   BLIND DATE. A bag grab.
   — When you expect to meet a vision and she turns out to to be a sight.

DAVENPORT. The seat of emotion.   *Anon.*

57

DAVIS, JEFF. A rebel rouser.

DAWN. A kind of backward sunset.
George Templeton Strong

DAY. There are some 500-odd days in a year, such as: Share with Ot ers Day, Make a Will Day, Own Your Own Home Day, National Fish Day, ad infinitum.
National Retail Dry Goods Association Calendar
— One good turn of the earth.
— A world revolution.
OFF DAY. The one that follows a day off. Anon.
DAYDREAM. A movie made while you wait.

DEACON. A constipated Christian. Anon., Jr.
— The lowest form of Christian. Anon., Jr. (British Division)
— A mass of inflammable material placed in a prominent position to warn people. Anon., Jr.

DEATH. A fate worse than life.
— A low chemical trick played on everybody except sequoia trees. J. J. Furnas
— A sure cure for insomnia.
— The conquering worm. Edgar Allan Poe
— The reward for living. Harry Ruby
— A leap in the dark. William Brodie
— A breath-taking experience.
— The one thing no one can survive. Oscar Wilde
— Life's last practical joke. Stuart Palmer
— Tax relief.
— Patrick Henry's second choice. Cynic's Cyclopaedia
DEATH RAY. The look one woman gives another who is wearing an identical outfit. The Wyatt Way

DEB. A ripe tomato surrounded by lettuce. Louis Nizer
DEBUTANTE. A butterfly in a power dive. Fred Runyon
— A gal who climbs the social ladder—lad by lad.
DEBUTANTES. Barebacks with greenbacks. Bob Hope

DEBARK. To peel a tree.

DEBATE. Babble instead of battle. *Don Quinn**

DE BERGERAC, CYRANO. An early ghost writer. *E. B. White*

DEBONAIR. The Park Avenue version of dapper.

DEBT. What you know you owe.
   DEBT-RIDDEN. Out to the people you're into.
Leonard Neubauer*

DECALCOMANIA. A particular form of insanity. *Anon., Jr.*

DECAPITATION. The sincerest form of capital punishment.

DEFEATISM. Saying die.

DEFENDANT. A man who has mislaid a chorus girl. *Anon.*

DEFICIT. The amount you didn't expect to lose.

DEFINITION. A statement intended to put a word in its place.
   DEFINITIZE (Pentagonese). Signifying the act of exhuming
    a "finalized" decision when Congress demands an au-
    topsy. *Russell Baker*

DELAY. The greatest remedy for anger. *Seneca*

DELIRIUM TREMENS. The wages of gin.

DELPHI. A wise crack on Parnassus.

DE LUXE. Mediocre in a big way.

DEMAGOGUE. A man who sways both ends against the middle.
Leonard Neubauer*
— A vessel from which one drinks beer.
Anon., Jr. (British Division)

DEMOCRACY. Government by popular ignorance.
Elbert Hubbard
— Government by amateurs. *Maxwell Anderson*
— Liberty plus groceries. *Maury Maverick*
— The principle that every person who is free, white, twenty-
  one, born in this country, and never caught out of step is
  entitled to choose the lesser of two evils.

— A form of government that substitutes election by the incompetent many for appointment by the corrupt few.

George Bernard Shaw

— A form of government in which it is permitted to wonder aloud what the country could do under first-class management.

Senator Soaper

DEMON. The devil, with turpentine on his tail.

DENTAL PARLOR. A drawing room.   *Anon.*

DEPRESSION. That period when we have to get along without those things our grandparents never dreamed of having.

Mike Connolly

— A dent in the dinner pail.

DESERT (v.). To leave without leave.

DESERT (N.). The sand which is here.   *George Bernard Shaw*

DESERTION. The poor man's divorce.   *Arthur Garfield Hays*

DESK. A waste basket with drawers.   *Wall Street Journal*

DESPOTISM. The right to be wrong.

DETECTIVE. A dealer in squealers.
— A man who earns his living by the sweat of his browbeating.
DETECTIVE STORY. A puzzle of people.

DETOUR. Something that lengthens your mileage, diminishes your gas, and strengthens your vocabulary.

Oliver Herford

— The roughest distance between two points.   *Anon.*

DIAGNOSTICIAN. A traffic cop to direct ailing people.

Will Rogers

DIALECT. A manner of speaking.

DIALOGUE. Prefabricated conversation.
— Penance inflicted by an author upon the actors, and by the actors upon the audience.

DIAPER. The eternal triangle.
— Trousers worn during the age of indiscretion.

DIAPHRAGM. A muscular partition separating disorders of the chest from disorders of the bowels.   *Ambrose Bierce*

DICKEY. A false front.

DICTAPHONE. A device to give homely stenographers an even break.

DICTATOR. A self-madman.   *Anon.*
DICTATORSHIP. General poverty relieved by enthusiasm and maintained by terror.   *Anon.*
— A government under which everything which is not prohibited is compulsory.   *Sergei Arutunoff*

DICTIONARY. A guide to the spelling of words, which can be located if you know how to spell them.
— A catalogue of grunts, explained by other grunts.
DICTIONARY, LEFT-HANDED. A dictionary into which a left-handed monkey wrench has been thrown.

DIDO. The same, and is usually represented by Dido marks.
Anon., Jr.

DIE. To stop sinning suddenly.   *Elbert Hubbard*

DIE-HARD. A man who worships the very ground his head's in.   *Bill Stern*

DIET. Doing without the dishes your doctor doesn't like.
— A strait jacket for the appetite.
— A system of starving yourself to death just so you can live a little longer.   *Jan Murray*
DIETING. One time when a man is happy to see his spare tire go flat.   *Joe Mah*

DIGESTION. The conversion of victuals into virtues.
Ambrose Bierce
DYSPEPSIA. The conversion of victuals into vices.
Ambrose Bierce

DIGNITY. Window dressing for a vacant store.
— Having stuffing instead of guts.

DILIGENCE. The mother of good luck.
                    *Cervantes and/or Benjamin Franklin
                    and/or Samuel Smiles*

DILLY-DALLY. To shilly-shally.

DILUTE. To take away by adding.

DINER. The car at the other end of the train.
                                        Weare Holbrook

DIPLOMA. A transfer to nowhere, issued at the end of the
line.

DIPLOMACY. Lying in state.   *Oliver Herford*
— Activity that isn't too hard on the brain, but hell on the
feet.   *Former Ambassador Charles G. Dawes*
    — (It depends on which you use.)
                    Former Ambassador Henry P. Fletcher
— The art of letting someone else have your own way. *Anon.*
— The art of saying "nice doggie" until you can find a rock.
                                                Anon.
— The art of putting one's foot down without treading on
anyone's toes.   *Patricia Stone*

DIPLOMAT. A stiff caller.
— A rabbit in a silk hat.
— A ward politician with a frock coat.
                            Gen. Smedley D. Butler
— A person who is appointed to avert situations that would
never occur if there were no diplomats. Hartford *Courant*
— A man who puts off until tomorrow what he can do today.
                            Dr. Hugo Riesenfeld°
— One who can yawn with his mouth closed. *College Humor*
— A man who remembers a woman's birthday, but not her
age.   *Anon. collegian*
— A man who can convince his wife she'd look stout in a
fur coat.   *Northwestern Bell*

DIRECTOR (Hollywood). The man who wants those sea gulls to wheel by the camera one by one.   *Morton Thompson**
— A manic depressive on the upswing.   *Archie Mayo*
— A movie hero who's lost his hair.

DIRT. Something in the wrong place.   *Lord Palmerston*
DIRT FARMER. One who thinks that everyone is doing him dirt.   *J. P. McEvoy*

DISARMAMENT. Agreement between nations to scuttle all weapons that are obsolete.

DISCORD. Noise out of place.

DISCRETION. Putting two and two together and keeping your mouth shut.
— A gift that comes to a person after he's too old for it to do him any good.   *Anon.*
— The art of closing your eyes to a situation before someone closes them for you.   *Earl Wilson*

DISHONORABLE. Any action committed by a competitor.
Elbert Hubbard

DISILLUSIONMENT. Going back for another look at your childhood sweetheart.   *Harry Ruby*

DISINFECTANT. A smell that is a greater smell than the original smell.   *Anon., Jr.*

DISINHERIT. To leave great sums of money to lawyers.
Elbert Hubbard

DISK JOCKEY. A guy who's paid a fortune to sit before a mike, separate good records from bad records, and then play the bad ones.   *Anon.*
— A man who gives phonograph records the needle.

DISSATISFACTION. The cause of all unrest.
Our Darktown Press
DISTANCE. A place to preserve heroes.

DISTANT RELATIVES. The best kind, and the further the better.
Kin Hubbard

DISTRIBUTION. An instrument something like a sieve by which the world's hands try to get food to the world's mouth.

DIVIDEND. A leak in the profit system.

DIVINE, FATHER. God—with pockets. *Art Arthur*

DIVORCE. The past tense of marriage. *Anon.*
— A hash made of domestic scraps. *Ed Wynn*
 DIVORCEE. A woman who gets richer by decrees.
The Houghton Line

DOCTOR. One who kills you today to prevent you from dying tomorrow. *Punch*
— The only man who hasn't a guaranteed cure for a cold.
Anon.
— The middleman between the bird with the big bill and the guy with the big sickle. *Don Quinn*
— A man who tells you if you don't cut something out, he will. *Frank Rossiter*
— The best doctor is the one you run for and can't find.
Diderot

DODO. A bird that is nearly decent now. *Anon., Jr.*

DOG. An intelligent four-footed animal who walks around with some dope on the end of his leash. *Anon.*
 DOG CATCHER. A man with a seeing-dog eye.

DOGGEREL. Poetry without pedigree.

DOGMATISM. Puppyism grown up.

DOLDRUMS. A series of high rocks near the equator.
Anon., Jr. (British Division)

DOMESTIC SERVICE. Doing housework for $60 a week. (Doing it for nothing is called matrimony.) *The Bulletin*

DON JUAN. A second-story worker.
— A town in the West Indies. *Anon., Jr.*

DOOMSDAY. The first day of the weak.

DOORMAN. A genius who can open the door of your car with one hand, help you in with the other, and still have one left for the tip. *Dorothy Kilgallen*
— One who looks down on those above him.
Irish Confectionery Trade Journal

DOPE SHEET. Advice to dopes. *Don Quinn**

DOUBLE-DEALING. When you buy something wholesale to sell retail. *Anon., Jr.*

DOUBLE FEATURE. A program that enables you to sit through a picture you don't want to see, so you can see one you don't like. *Henry Morgan*
— Something that makes it impossible for you to come in in the middle of both pictures. *Morton Thompson*

DOUR. A sort of help, as in the hymn, "O God dour help in ages past." *Anon., Jr.*

DRAFT BOARD. The world's largest travel agency.

DREAM. The offspring of indigestion. *Anon.*
DREAMS. Moving pictures that you see when you're asleep.
Anon., Jr.

DRESDEN. The capital of China. *Anon., Jr. (British Division)*

DRESS. Woman's constant endeavor to improve on her skin.

DRIVE-IN THEATRE. A parking lot where you find young couples and old movies. *Phil Foster*

DRIVER, CAREFUL. One who looks in both directions when he passes a red light. *Ralph Marterie*

DRIZZLE. A drip that's going steady. *Anon.*

DRUGSTORE. A telephone with a business attached.

DRUNK. Feeling sophisticated but unable to pronounce it.
Anon.
— A nightmare from which one awakens to learn it was real.
— The future of drink. *Anon., Jr.*
DRUNK DRIVING. Putting the quart before the hearse.
DRUNKARD. A person who tries to pull himself out of trouble with a corkscrew. *Ed Baldwin*

DSWARDATELATRUTHANUTHINBUTATRUTHSOHELPYAGOD! Form of swearing heard in courtrooms.

DUCKY. The wife of a duke. *Anon., Jr.*

DUET. A co-opera.

DUKE OF MARLBOROUGH. A great general who always commenced every battle with a fixed determination in his mind to win or lose. *Anon., Jr.*

DULLES, JOHN FOSTER. The greatest salesman of paper moons in the history of that branch of the merchandising industry known as diplomacy. *William V. Shannon*

DUMPLING. A bloated biscuit.

DUN. What you do to avoid being done.

DUSK. Little bits of stuff that fly about in the air.
Anon., Jr. (British Division)

DUST. Mud with the juice squeezed out. *Foolish Dictionary*
DUST BOWL. Land devastated by a grime wave.

DUTY. What one expects from others. *Oscar Wilde*
— Refraining from wine, women, and money.
Anon. policeman

DWARF. A jockey with a long beard. *Jack Benny*

DYNAMO. A machine that makes dynamite and other explosions. *Anon., Jr.*

E

E.G. Egg sample. *Anon., Jr. (British Division)*

EARLY RISERS. People who are conceited in the morning and stupid in the afternoon. *Rose Henniker Heaton*

EARLY WINTER. Novembrrrrrr. *Edward B. Smith*

EARTH. A water-covered sphere, crusted here and there with continents upon which there is the fragile green hue of life. *Walter Sullivan*
— A planet that had its chance.
— A dying cinder. *A. Hyatt Verrill*
EARTHQUAKE. Nature's own subversive movement.

EASY CHAIR. The hardest one to find empty. *Danotto*

EAVESDROPPER. Adam. *Anon., Jr.*
— An icicle. *Anon., Jr.*
— A kind of bird. *Anon., Jr.*

ECHO. Back talk from Mother Nature. *Dude's Dictionary*
— The son of the rock. *Ossian*
— The perfect comeback.

ECLIPSE. J. P. Morgan foreclosing on the sun. *Al Boasberg*

ECONOMY. The art of spending money without getting any fun out of it. *Anon.*
— Going without something you do want, in case you should someday want something which you probably won't like.
Anthony Hope
ECONOMIC LAG. The gap between the bread basket and the dinner pail.

ECONOMIST. A side-show guess-your-weight merchant with a college degree.　*Judge*

— A guy with a Phi Beta Kappa key on one end of his watch chain and no watch on the other end.
Alben W. Barkley

— A man who states the obvious in terms of the incomprehensible.　*Alfred A. Knopf*

POLITICAL ECONOMY. Getting votes for as little money as possible.　*Anon.*

RIGID ECONOMY. A dead Scotchman.　*Will Rogers*

ECSTASY. Happiness with its clothes off.

ECTOPLASM. The life blood of a ghost.

EDEN, ANTHONY. A dirty port in Suez, mostly used for coaling.
Anon., Jr. (British Division)

EDIBLE. Good to eat, and wholesome to digest; as a worm to a toad, a toad to a snake, a snake to a pig, a pig to a man, and a man to a worm.　*Ambrose Bierce*

EDITOR. A man who knows what he wants, but doesn't know what it is.　*Walter Davenport, editor*

— A person employed on a newspaper, whose business it is to separate the wheat from the chaff, and to see that the chaff is printed.　*Elbert Hubbard*

ASSISTANT CITY EDITOR. A mouse learning to be a rat.
Anon. reporter

CITY EDITOR. A reporter whose legs have gone back on him.
Anon. reporter

EDITORIAL DEPARTMENT. The staff that prepares a newspaper's sustaining program.

EDUCATION. One of the few things a person is willing to pay for and not get.　*William Lowe Bryan*

— The concealment of ignorance.　*Anon.*

— Teaching a child how to talk—and then how to keep quiet.
Emporia *Gazette*

— The development of the memory at the expense of the imagination.　*Owen Johnson*

— What's left over after you've forgotten the facts.
Memphis Transit News
— The battle against Nature.
— Something that enables you to get into more expensive
  trouble. Judge
— What a man gets when he sits in his living room with a
  group of teen-agers.
— Reeling and writhing and different branches of arithmetic
  —ambition, distraction, uglification, and derision.
Lewis Carroll

EEL. A sea-going snake. John Kiernan

EFFEMINACY. The lilies' guild.

EFFICIENCY. The art of lost motion.

EFFIGY. A scarecrow with a bad personality.

EGG. A fowl ball.
— An adventure. Oscar Wilde
— A day's work for a hen.
— A bird's home town.

EGO. The personality as the center of the universe.
   EGOTISM. A case of mistaken nonentity. Barbara Stanwyck
   — The anesthetic given by a kindly nature to relieve the
     pain of being a damned fool. Bellamy Brooks
   — An alphabet of one letter. London Truth
   — I-dolatry.
   — I soar.
   EGOTIST. A guy who's always me-deep in conversation.
Bill Bertolotti

EIGHTEEN. Old enough to know everything.

EINSTEIN, ALBERT. The man who took a stitch in time.
Don Quinn*

ELBOW. A joint that provides a hand-to-mouth existence.

ELECTROCUTION. Burning at the stake with all modern improvements.

ELEPHANT. A square animal with a tail in front and behind.
Anon., Jr. (British Division)

ELF. A fairy, j.g.

ELK. A deer whose mother was frightened by Jimmy Durante.

ELOCUTION. The execution of eloquence.
— A thing that people were killed with in some states.
Anon., Jr.

ELOPEMENT. Love laughing at locksmiths.

ELOQUENCE. Saying the proper thing and stopping.
Stanley Link

EMBALMING. Cheating the early worm.

EMBEZZLEMENT. Bankers away!
EMBEZZLER. One who soils the till.

EMPHASIS. Putting more distress in one place than another.
Anon., Jr.

EMOTION. The back-seat driver of the mind.

EMU. The name of the noise made by a cat. *Anon., Jr.*

ENEMY. A pal who could steal your wife—but won't.
*Harry Hirshfield**

ENFORCEMENT. The difference between law and order.

ENGAGEMENT. In love, a period of occupation without possession.

ENGINEER. A man who can take a theory and put wheels on it.
— (Railroad) A man who has ridden far and gotten nowhere.
E. B. White

ENGLAND. A country with a government that is a limited mockery. *Anon., Jr.*

— A country with a dozen different licensing systems and only one fish sauce. *Anon.*

— An island entirely surrounded by hot water.

London *Opinion*

ENGLISH. Anglo-Saxon after the French got through with it.

ENGLISHMAN. A strong being who takes a cold bath in the morning and talks about it for the rest of the day.

Ellen Wilkinson

— One who dines by himself in a room filled with other hermits. *James Fenimore Cooper*

— A creature who thinks he is being virtuous when he is only being uncomfortable. *George Bernard Shaw*

ENIGMA. The mother of bewilderment.

ENTOURAGE. A screen of stooges.

ENTREPRENEUR. A man who has been in business a lot of times. *Fritz B. Burns*

ENVY. The mean man's gratitude. *Bulwer*

EPIC. A motion picture which can be split for intermission.

— A double feature on a single subject.

EPICURE. A poet who writes epics. *Anon., Jr.*

EPIDEMIC. A needle the doctor uses to put medicine in your arm. *Anon., Jr.*

EPIGRAM. A remark that is too good to be true.

— A half truth so stated as to irritate the person who believes the other half. *Shailer Mathews*

— A wisecrack that has played Carnegie Hall. *Oscar Levant**

BRILLIANT EPIGRAM. A solemn platitude gone to a masquerade ball. *Lionel Strachey*

EPILEPSY. The survival of the fit.

EPISTLE. The wife of an apostle. *Anon., Jr.*

---

* A wisecracker who has played Carnegie Hall.

EPITAPH. A belated advertisement for a line of goods that
has been permanently discontinued. *Irvin S. Cobb*
— The last word. *Homer Croy*
— Here lies my wife Sallie; let her lie;
She's at peace, and so am I.
— A statement that usually lies above about the one who lies
beneath. *Foolish Dictionary*
— Under this sod lies John Round,
Who was lost at sea and never found.
— Postponed compliments. *Elbert Hubbard*
— A short sarcastic poem *Anon., Jr.*
— A description of the dead.

EPITHET. A description of the living.

EQUALITY. The right, granted by the Constitution, of rich
and poor, black and white, to bathe in champagne and
winter on the Riviera. *Leo C. Rosten*

EQUATOR. A menagerie lion running around the earth's middle. *Anon., Jr.*

EQUIPAGE. Stolen goods. *Shakespeare*

ERG. When people are playing football and you want them
to do their best, you erg them on. *Anon., Jr.*

ERRATA. A typographical confession.

ERSATZ. The enemy's breakfast food.

ERUDITION. Having read a book the other fellow never
heard of.

ESAU. A man who wrote fables and sold his copyright for a
mess of potash. *Anon., Jr. (British Division)*

ESCAPE. A slave's business.
    ESCAPIST. A person who looks the facts of life in the back
    of the neck. *Cedric Belfrage*

ESKIMOS. Arctic natives who are only a few Lapps from civilization.
— God's frozen people.   *Edward Weyer*

ESPERANTO. The combination salad of language.
— Reversing Babel.

ETC. A sign used to make others believe you know more than you do.   *Anon.*

ETCHING. A ticklish feeling.   *Anon., Jr.*

ETERNAL TRIANGLE. A wife, a husband and a hairdo.

ETERNITY. The Sunday of Time.   *Elbert Hubbard*
— Paying for a $700 piano on the installment plan.   *Life*

ETIQUETTE. The noise you don't make while eating soup.
                    Anon.
— Learning to yawn with your mouth closed.
                    "It Pays to Be Ignorant"

EUNUCH. An old refrain.   *Leonard Neubauer**
— One who is cut off from temptation.
— The favorite instrument of the ancient Arabians. *Anon., Jr.*

EUROPE. A collection of countries that want to be left a loan.
— The lost continent.
— A peninsula occupying the northwestern portion of Asia.
                    Raymond Mortimer

EVE. Madam Adam.
— The first sin that came into the world.   *Anon., Jr.*

EVOLUTION. A disreputable episode on one of the minor planets.   *Lord Balfour*
— An unsuccessful attempt to produce a human being.

EXAGGERATION. Truth that has lost its temper.
                    Kahlil Gibran

EXCAVATE. To hollow out, e.g., "Our baby excavates when he gets hurt." *Anon., Jr. (British Division)*

EXCELSIOR. Long sawdust. *Anon., Jr.*

EXCISE. A mode or manner by which authorities extort money from inhabitants for the king to pay the national debt.
Anon., Jr. (British Division)
— It is good for us to have excise in the open air, as the air vibrates through our muscells.
Anon., Jr. (British Division)

EXCLAMATION POINT. A period that's blown its top.
Stars & Stripes

EXCLUSIVENESS. A characteristic of recent riches, high society and the skunk. *Austin O'Malley*

EXCOMMUNICATE. To tell a man to deal with God direct.
— To stop writing. *Anon., Jr.*

EXECUTIVE. A man who talks golf around the office all morning and business around the golf course all afternoon.

EXHIBITIONIST. One who strips without teasing.

EXISTENCE. A lease on life.

EXPEDIENCY. The art of rushing to the defense of the winning side. *Amiel*

EXPERIENCE. The name everyone gives to his mistakes.
Oscar Wilde
— What you have left after everything else is gone. *Anon.*
— What you've got when you're too old to get a job.
Leon Abramson
— A marvelous thing that enables you to recognize a mistake whenever you make it again. *Franklin P. Jones*
— Experience . . . a fine teacher, it's true,
But here's what makes me burn:
Experience is always teaching me
Things I'd rather not learn! *Ethel M. Wegert*
— The mistakes we like to remember.

EXPERT. A man who avoids errors as he sweeps on to the grand fallacy. *B. Stollberg*

— One who knows too much about one subject.

— A man who has stopped thinking. *Frank Lloyd Wright*

— A guy who can complicate the hell out of something simple. *Anon.*

— A guy from out of town. *David Flexer**

EXPOSITION. An overgrown department store, usually opened a year or two behind time. *Foolish Dictionary*

EXTRAVAGANCE. The way the other fellow spends his money. *Harry Thompson*

EYELIDS. Draperies for the conscience. *Albert A. Brandt*

F

FABLE. Something that should have happened to a dog.

FABULOUS. "We haven't seen anything like it in the last half an hour."
Macy's

FACE. A screen for the mind.
Anon.
— With most people, a convenience rather than an ornament.
Oliver Wendell Holmes

FACETIOUS. A term used to denote the followers of Mussolini.
Anon., Jr.

FACT. A grain of sense.
— The hardest thing in this world to get.
Walter Yost, editor-in-chief, Encyclopaedia Britannica

FAD. Something that goes in one era and out the other.
American Legion

FADEOUT (Hollywood). The kindest cut of all.
Leonard Neubauer*

FAILURE. The path of least persistence. *Associated Grocers*
— One who has succeeded in failing.

FAINTS. A barricade of wood or brick. *Charlestonese*

FAIRY-TALE. A horror story to prepare children for the newspapers.

FAITH. An illogical belief in the occurrence of the improbable.
H. L. Mencken
— That quality which enables us to believe what we know to be untrue.
Anon., Jr.
— The quality that enables you to eat blackberry jam on a picnic without looking to see whether the seeds move.
Current Medical Digest

76

FALSEHOOD. The mother-in-law of invention.
— A varnished truth.

FALSIE. A device to make a mountain out of a molehill.

FAME. A bubble that often comes from blowing your own
horn. *Bishop Berry*
— The aggregate of all the misunderstandings that collect
around a new name. *Rainer Maria Rilke*
— Chiefly a matter of dying at the right moment.
Bud Walters
— The prolonging of neighborhood gossip. *Jim Tully**

FAN. A thing you brush the warm off with.
Anon., Jr. (British Division)
— (Movie) A person who goes to the movies on purpose.
FAN-MAGAZINE WRITER. A slobber sister.
FAN MAIL. A sort of hippopotamus that, having pushed
one's front door open with his nose, squats with a drip-
ping smile in a pool on one's hearthrug. Its impulse is
charming, but one doesn't quite know what the devil
to do with him. *John Barrymore*

FANATIC. A lunatic with a hobby.
— One who can't change his mind and won't change the
subject. *Winston Churchill*
FANATICISM. Redoubling your effort when you have forgotten your aim. *George Santayana*

FAN TAN. A Chinaman's chance.

FARM. An irregular patch of nettles, bounded by short-term
notes, containing a fool and his wife who didn't know
enough to stay in the city. *S. J. Perelman*
— A place where the folks get up to see the Late Late Show.
Earl Wilson
FARMER. A man who grows cotton, wheat, corn, and
desperate.
— A handy man with a sense of humus. *E. B. White*

GENTLEMAN FARMER. One who has more hay in the bank than in the barn. *Anon.*
— One who raises his hat in a grain elevator.
Charlie McCarthy
FARMING. Growing enough food so that by selling it all at a good price, enough of it can be bought back to feed the family.

FASCISM. An army on the march. *Mussolini, 1930*
— Capitalism plus murder. *Upton Sinclair*
FASCIST. A man who kills because he can't argue. *Anon.*

FASHION. A racket for selling clothes. *Anon.*
— A clothes-horse show. *Carolyn Wells*
— A form of ugliness so intolerable that we have to alter it every six months. *Oscar Wilde*
— Something that goes in one year and out the other.
Tommy Graham
— Something that goes out of style as soon as most people have one. *Sylvia Strum Bremer*
— A woman's compromise between the admitted desire to dress and the unadmitted desire to undress. *Lin Yutang*
— What one wears oneself; what is unfashionable is what other people wear. *Oscar Wilde*
FASHIONABLE. An uncertain balance between the desire to be exclusive and the pleasure of being imitated.

FAT. Dull. *Shakespeare*

FATALIST. A party that thinks you're doin' him a deep pussonal favor when you kill him. *Irvin S. Cobb*

FATE. The secret map of chance.

FATHER. A banker by nature. *French proverb*
— The kin you love to touch. *College Humor*
— A guy who is working his son's way through college.
Alan Dale
— One who strikes a child only in self-defense.

— A man whose daughter marries a man vastly her inferior mentally but then gives birth to unbelievably brilliant grandchildren. *Anon.*

FATHER'S DAY. Like Mother's Day, only you don't spend as much. *Marvin Hodas*

FAULKNER, WILLIAM. Poe in a hand-me-down suit.
Jim Tully*

FAWN. A gazelle with an inferiority complex. *Fred Allen*

FEAR. Ignorance.
— Knowledge.
— The tax that conscience pays to guilt. *Anon.*

FEAST. A meal at another's expense.

FEATHER-BEDDING. Providing jobs soft enough to die down on.

FEDERAL AID. A system of making money taken from the people look like a gift when handed back. *Carl Workman*

FEDERAL RESERVE. A reserve where the federal employees hunt wild game. *Anon., Jr.*

FEMALE. One who believes if you charge it, it's not spending, and if you add a cherry to it, it's not intoxicating.
Jack Pearl

— The fee of the male.
FEMININE WILE. Keeping a man at arm's length by a hair's breadth. *Wall Street Journal*

FENCING. A game of chess accomplished on foot. *Anon.*

FERVOR. Fever with a purpose.

FETISH. It is applied to persons who seem to have a gay air, as if they were going to a fete.
Anon., Jr. (British Division)

FEZ. An African city which might have been dreamed up by Edgar Allan Poe. *John Gunther*

FICTION. Those books which are fixed on the shelves and are not to be moved; nonfiction are not fixed and may be moved at will. *Anon., Jr.*

FIFTH COLUMNIST. An enemy who is invisible when you are sitting next to him at dinner, but whom you think you see under the bed. *Edmond Taylor*

FIGHT ARENA. A punch bowl.

FIGHT MANAGER. A man with a license to make a living while committing vagrancy. *Jimmy Cannon*

FILET MIGNON. An opera by Puccini. *Anon., Jr.*

FILIBUSTER. Freedom of screech.

FILING CABINET. A place to lose things alphabetically. *Anon.*

FINALE. A Mexican delicacy wrapped in a corn husk.
Anon., Jr.

FINALIZE (Bureaucratese). Signifying formal adoption of a decision, policy or program, with tacit agreement that it be given a quiet burial, or "implemented." *Russell Baker*

FINANCE. The art of passing money from one hand to another until it finally disappears.

FINGER-MAN. A two-legged pointer.

FIRE. A chemical process used in cooking, heating, and getting a new start in business.
FIRE HORSE (Obsolete). A spark plug.
FIREMAN. A guy who knocks on a door with an ax. *Anon.*
VOLUNTEER FIREMAN. A redhot with a red hat.

FISH. The only thing that smells worse than a guest on the third day. *Spanish proverb*
FISHING. A jerk at one end of the line waiting for a jerk at the other end. *Galen Drake*
— A delusion entirely surrounded by liars and old clothes.
Don Marquis

FISSURE. A man who sells fish. *Anon., Jr. (British Division)*

FIT. An accident in a tailor's shop. *Cynic's Cyclopaedia*

FLAG. The trademark of a nation.

FLAME. A man who is about to make an ash of himself.

FLATTER. To feed with an empty spoon. *Italian proverb*
  FLATTERER. One who says things to your face that he wouldn't say behind your back. *G. Millington*
  FLATTERY. Telling the other guy what he already thinks of himself. *Hal Wilshire*
  — Something nice someone tells you about yourself that you wish were true. *Frank Malester*
  — Soft soap. *Anon.*
  SOFT SOAP. 90 per cent lye. *Anon.*
  — Like perfume, to be smelled, not swallowed.
      Josh Billings
  — What really flatters a man is that you think him worth flattering. *George Bernard Shaw*

FLEA. The bravest of all the creatures of God, if ignorance of fear were courage. *Mark Twain*

FLIRT. A woman who believes that it's every man for herself.
      Country Gentlewoman
  FLIRTING. Wishful winking. *Sid Caesar*

FLOOD. A river too big for its bridges.

FLOOR. The only thing that will stop falling hair. *Anon.*

FLOW. What you stand on in a house. *Charlestonese*

FLU. An ill wind that makes everybody blow good. *Lisa Kirk*

FLUKE. A fish so dumb, it's five years old before it learns to swim. *William Frawley*

FLY. A lunch-counter irritant.
  FLY SCREEN. An arrangement for keeping flies in the house.
      Foolish Dictionary

Focus. A thing like a mushroom, but if you eat it, you will feel differently from a mushroom, for focuses is poison.

Anon., Jr.

Fog. Stuff that's dangerous to drive in—especially if it's mental. *F. G. Kernan*

Foible. A tale or story which generally has a moral, as in Aesop's Foibles. *Anon., Jr.*

Folk Dancing. Making "hey" while the moon shines. *Anon.*

Food (Army). Sad Snack. *L. Martin Courtney II*

Fool. A man who uses the brains God gave him.
Foolhardiness. Scorning warning.

Football. A sport that bears the same relation to education that bullfighting does to agriculture. *Elbert Hubbard*
Football Game. A contest where a spectator takes four quarters to finish a fifth.
Football Season. The only time of the year when a man can walk down the street with a blonde on one arm and a blanket on the other without encountering raised eyebrows. *Anon.*

Footnote. Like running downstairs to answer the doorbell during the first night of marriage. *John Barrymore*
— Tedious information set aside where it can be easily skipped.*

---

* The first use of the word as meaning a note or comment added at the foot of the text was in 1841, according to the Shorter Oxford English Dictionary, although such notes were certainly a typographical practice before then. The author has a copy of the New York edition of *The Great Metropolis* (meaning London), published in 1837, which has such explanatory addenda on a number of pages. He also has a book printed in 1749 containing footnotes in the best modern style; it is *L'Art de conserver sa santé*, a French rendering in verse of the medical maxims of Salerne, in which clarifications of certain Latin words are so placed at the feet of the pages. The French have a word for this, but naturally

FOREWORD. An author's apology.

FORGER. A fellow who gives a check a bad name.
                                    Prairie du Chien, Wisc., *Courier*

FORGIVENESS. God's business.   *Heinrich Heine*
— The fragrance the violet sheds on the heel that has crushed
    it.   *Anon. asylum inmate quoted by Mark Twain*

FORTUNATE. Better off than you are.

FORTUNETELLER. A person who tells you about the past and
    the future for a present.

---

it is not "footnote." At this period in England, however, footnotes
seem to have been placed at the sides of the pages (as, e.g., in
The Biographia Britannica, 1744, another book the author has).
It would be too much to expect sidenotes to be called footnotes,
and indeed, during the seventeenth and eighteenth centuries, the
word "marginal" was in use to mean a note in the margin; it did
not acquire its financial connotation until 1887, sometime between
the unveiling of the Statue of Liberty and the Great Blizzard.
It is believed by some that the French custom of placing added
information at the bottom of the page rather than at the side at-
tracted the interest of Benjamin Franklin when he was abroad and
was by him introduced to the colonies, from whence it was picked
up by English printers. This is supposition, however. It would
appear from an examination of Franklin's writings in their earlier
editions that the footnote was at first an editor's privilege, and
that an author was expected to say all he had to say in the text
and then shut up. In the nineteenth century American writers
rebelled at this practice and began to anticipate and disarm their
future editors by making their own footnotes as they went along,
signing them "Author." This forced further emendators to identify
themselves by "ed.," or "Joe," or whatever their name was; the
more dignified would use initials, as "Q.E.D." Nowadays pedants
find it so difficult to keep pace with what they are writing about
that the custom has arisen of dating the footnotes, thus giving a
picture in rather slow motion of the unfolding of the author's
mind. As to when the designation "footnote" was adopted, there
seems no record except the date of 1841 given above. A happier
term would have been "footlight," but that term was pre-empted
in 1836 by the theatre to designate the lights placed at the front
of the stage to keep the actors from seeing where the vegetables
were coming from. P.S.: This was a footnote.

FORTY. The old age of youth. Fifty is the youth of old age.
Victor Hugo

— The most difficult age for a woman to pass. Sometimes it
takes ten years. *Jackie Kannon*

FOUNDING FATHERS. Dead revolutionists. *Leo C. Rosten*

FOUNTAIN PEN. A writing instrument that works marvelously
in the store.

FOUR SEASONS. Salt, pepper, mustard, and vinegar. *Anon., Jr.*

FOX. A wolf who sends flowers. *Jacob M. Braude*
FOX HUNT. The unspeakable in pursuit of the uneatable.
Oscar Wilde
FOX TROT. A slow and circuitous walk, slightly impeded by
a member of the opposite sex. *Lord Balfour*

FRANCE. A country where the impossible always happens and
the inevitable never does. *The New York Times*

FRATERNITY HOUSE. A place where a long-playing record is
lucky to last two days. *Voo Doo*

FREE. Without money.
FREE PRESS. One hundred men imposing their prejudices
on one hundred million. *Leo C. Rosten*
FREE SPEECH. The right to talk back to the radio.
FREE VERSE. Verse written without rhyme or reason.

FREEBOOTER. An amateur soccer player. *Anon.*

FREEDOM. The animal kingdom's improvement on the vegetable kingdom.
FREEDOM OF THE PRESS. The right to say anything you
want to in print if you have the money to buy the press,
paper, and news service.

FRENCHMAN. Just an Italian with a bad temper.
Dennis McEvoy

FRIDAY. The day of the Christian week when God created fish.

  GOOD FRIDAY. The fellow who did Robinson Crusoe's housework. *Pathfinder*

FRIEND. Somebody who knows all about you—and likes you just the same. *Contact*
— One who will listen to your troubles without telling his.
— A present you give yourself. *Robert Louis Stevenson*
— A name for a more constant acquaintance *Horace Walpole*
— A guy who has the same enemies you have.
                            Walter Winchell
  FRIENDS. People who borrow my books and set wet glasses on them. *Edwin Arlington Robinson*
  FRIENDSHIP. A holy passion, so sweet and steady and loyal and enduring in its nature that it will last through a whole lifetime, if not asked to lend money. *Mark Twain*
  — Little more than honor among rogues. *Thoreau*

FRUGALITY. Being mean to yourself.

FUGITIVE. One who has the courage of his convictions.

FUN. Joy unrefined.
— Like insurance—the older you get the more it costs.
                       Chicago *Herald-American*

FUNERAL. A coming-out party for a ghost.
— The last bedtime story.

FUR COAT. A second-hand garment.

FURNITURE. Structures to support the human body in various positions.

FUTURE. The best thing about it is that it only can come one day at a time. *Anon. old lady*

G

G. The original Latin name of the letter G was *gay*, which probably explains the fall of the Roman Empire.

That was the beginning of the fallacy that G, being the seventh letter in the alphabet of most of the civilized nations, is also the luckiest letter. Anyone with nothing but a G-string to his name knows different.

G is just a common or garden letter with a curved back and a toothpick in his mouth, standing on the corner of F Street and Avenue H, watching the Girls go by. By all the laws of initialdom he may think himself some Guy, but there aren't many thrilling things G represents . . . except perhaps garters, gamma rays, Jehovah-in-one syllable, a rare tropical carrion crow called the gallinazo, germs, Germany, the science of goniometry, and something no worse than a bad cold.

Nature obviously never intended a great many of her G-men to turn out to be G-whizzers. The most renowned specimens in the Gee-Gee stalls of fame seem to be that knightly narcissist, Sir Galahad, M. Gandhi in his spiritual jaegers, King Gilgamesh of Ashurbanipal, a good staple line of popes named Gregory, a couple of Garcías (pana-tela-shaped), a gangster called Genghis Khan—they get in everywhere!—an old itinerant printer named Gutenberg without whom such weighty tomes as this would have been impossible.

Pretty nearly the nicest thing to be said for G is that it stands for genius—which is more than most families can do, and you can't entirely blame them—and for nature's biggest, hairiest and honestest biped, the gorilla, habitat Chicago.

In short, practically anything composed in the key of G is made up of grunts, groans and growing pains . . . like mine.   *Gilbert Gabriel*°

G.O.P. Grandfather's Old Party.

GABRIEL. The last minstrel.

GADGET. A luxury from the 5 & 10.

GAEL. A storm at sea. There was a gael in Shakespeare's *Tempest*.   *Anon., Jr.*

GAG WRITER. A man who sharpens old saws.

GALAHAD. A Boy Scout with a horse.
— A man who beat Ivory Soap by 56/100 per cent.

GALL. Something you have when you have nothing else.

GAMBLER. One who plays the fool.
  PROFESSIONAL GAMBLER. One who plays against the fool.
  GAMBLING. The sure way of getting nothing for something.
                                                           Wilson Mizner

GANDHI. Lawyer, doctor, beggar, thief, rich man, poor man, Indian chief.   *English proverb*

GANG. A vicious circle.

GANGES. The Swami river.

GARAGE. A ground-floor attic.

GARBAGE CAN. An example of collective noun.   *Anon., Jr.*

GARBO, GRETA. A deer, in the body of a woman, living resentfully in the Hollywood zoo. *Clare Boothe Brokaw Luce*

GARDENER. A man with a hinge in his back.   *Anon.*
  GARDEN. A thing of beauty and a job forever.   *Anon.*
  — Something that dies if you don't water it, and rots if you do.   Newark *Evening News*
  GARDENING. Man's effort to improve his lot.

GARNISHMENT. A court plaster.

GARTER. A rubber band with glamour.

GASOLINE. The odor of civilization.

GASTRITIS. Belch-schmertz. *Viola Brothers Shore**

GELDING. A stallion who had his tonsils taken out so he would
have more time to himself. *Anon., Jr.*

GEM. A sweet you spread on bread. It come otter a jaw.
New Yorkese

GENDER. The destruction of sex. *Anon., Jr.*
— The two genders are masculine and feminine. The mas-
culines are divided into temperate and intemperate and
feminines into frigid and torrid. *Anon., Jr.*

GENEALOGIST. One who traces your family as far back as
your money will go. *Anon.*
GENEALOGY. A kin game.

GENIUS. The brights' disease.
— The talent of a man who is dead. *Edmond de Goncourt*
— A man who shoots at something no one else can see, and
hits it. *Anon.*
— A man who can rewrap a new shirt and not have any pins
left over. *Dino Levi*
— A smart foreigner. *John Ely Burckard*
— Some other woman's husband. *Cosmo Sardo*
— A man who balances his budget. *Bob Levinson**
— An infinite capacity for not having to take pains.
Beerbohm Tree
— An infinite capacity for picking brains. *Anon., Jr.*
HOLLYWOOD GENIUS. A man who knows a good thing when
he sees it, provided someone else sees it first.
Cora Galenti

GENTLE. Unnatural.
GENTLEMAN. A man on a horse. *Spanish meaning*
— One who never hurts another's feelings unintentionally.
Oliver Herford
— A man who helps a woman across the street even if she
does need help. *Franklin P. Jones*

— A guy who wouldn't hit a woman with his hat on.
Fred Allen
— One who never heard the story before. *Austin O'Malley*

GERM. A little bug with influence.
GERMS. Very objectionable to men but a germ thinks of a man as only the swamp in which he has to live.
Don Marquis

GERMAN. A good fellow, maybe; but it is better to hang him.
Russian proverb
— The head man, i.e., "He's the german of the board."
New Yorkese

GHERKIN. A pretty pickle.

GHETTO. The first spot on the pogrom.

GHOST. A shadow of its former self.
GHOST WRITER. One who can write without moving his lips.

GHOUL. The Second Grave-digger.

GIBSON GIRL. A young lady whose waist you could span with your two hands—but she couldn't sit down in a tub.
George Ade

GIFT SHOP. A place where you can see all the things you hope your friends won't send you for Christmas.
Jack Woolsey

GIGGLE. A laugh that never made good. *Monte Prosser*

GIGOLO. A man who lives off the fat of the land.

GINGER ALE. A drink that tastes like your foot feels when it's asleep. *Anon.*

GIRAFFE. The highest form of animal life. *France Soir*

GIRDLE. A line tamer. *Walter Winchell*
— Something that keeps figures from telling the truth. *Anon.*
— A device that prevents an unfortunate situation from spreading. *Daddy Snooks*

GIRL. A Thing that (1) lights a cigarette just as the bus she's waiting for pulls up; (2) comes at you with an umbrella on a rainy day, swerves and doesn't poke until she sees the whites of your eyes; (3) tells the taxi where to stop, opens a handbag, takes out a pocketbook, closes the handbag, opens the pocketbook, takes out a change purse, closes the pocketbook, opens the change purse, closes the change purse and hands the cab driver a $20 bill . . . opens the change purse, puts in her change, closes the change purse, opens the pocketbook, puts in the change purse, closes the pocketbook, opens the handbag, puts in the pocketbook, closes the handbag, looks at the people waiting for the cab, has a new idea and gives the hack driver a new address two blocks down the street; (4) tells you that what you need is a good home-cooked dinner and when you get to her place she discovers she's out of booze and after you've gone out for a bottle and you both have a drink she says: "I can tell by your face you'd rather we went out to a restaurant."

Robert Sylvester

— A vision in the evening and a sight in the morning. *Anon.*

GIRLHOOD. Sixty pounds ago. *Ernest L. Meyer*

GIRLS. The ones that dance backward. *Bob Hope*

SMART GIRL. One who can hold a man at arm's length without losing her grip on him. *Anon.*

GLACIER. Frozen geography.

— A man who goes along the street with glass in his hand and puts it in windows. *Anon., Jr.*

GLADSTONE, WILLIAM E. A sophistical rhetorician, inebriated with the exuberance of his own verbosity and gifted with an egotistical imagination that can at all times command an interminable and inconsistent series of arguments to malign an opponent and glorify himself. *Disraeli*

GLAMOUR. What a movie gal has after the fashion designer, the fitter, the hairdresser, the make-up man, the electrician, the cameraman, the director, and the press agent have worked on her.

— When the value of the package exceeds that of the contents.   *Dr. Paul B. Popence*

GLAMOUR GIRL. One who has what it takes to take what you have.   *Air Mail*

GLAZIER. A man who runs down mountains.
                    Anon., Jr. (British Division)

GLORY. The reward for having a high quotient of annihilative efficiency.

GLOVE. A hand shoe.

GLUTTON. A person who takes the piece of French pastry you wanted.   *Anon.*

GO-CART. Transportation for a mad moment. *Jackson Parks**

GOATEE. A beard that's from Dixie.
— A whisper of a whisker.   *Dorothy Gulman**
— A small goat.   *Russell Patterson**

GOBLET. A small sailor.   *Judge*
— A small male turkey.   *Anon., Jr.*

GOD. The hero of a book called the Bible.   *Nelson Glueck*
— An explanation that saves an explanation.
— A reasoning being would lose his reason in attempting to account for the great phenomena of nature, had he not a Supreme Being to refer to; and well has it been said that, if there had been no God, mankind would have been obliged to imagine one.   *George Washington*
— A noted foreigner assisting the colonists in the Revolutionary War.   *Anon., Jr.*
— Like perpetual motion man's most unworkable invention.

GODFREY, ARTHUR. A performer who sings like a frog with a man in his throat.   *George Reim*

GOLD. A metal men dig out of holes for dentists and governments to put back in.   *Wall Street Journal*

GOLD DIGGER. A girl who breaks dates by going out with them.   *Anon.*

GOLDWYN, SAMUEL. A real-estate man with taste.
                                                    Martin Rackin

GOLF. A game in which one endeavors to control a ball with implements ill adapted for the purpose.   *Woodrow Wilson*
— A game where the ball always lies poorly; and the player well.   *Reader's Digest*
— A game in which a ball one and a half inches in diameter is placed on a ball 8,000 miles in diameter. The object is to hit the small ball but not the larger.
                                                    John Cunningham
— The only game which has a moral purpose and is definitely tinged with a touch of the spiritual. *Rev. Henry H. Shires*
— A game you play with your own worst enemy—yourself.
                                                    Mr. Dooley
GOLF CLUB. A place where the members try to break 80 on the course and 90 on the way home in their cars.
                                                    Anon.
GOLF COURSE. The result of God having a mouthful of spinach and sneezing.

GOOD. One of mankind's most inexplicable perversions.
                                                    Ingmar Bergman
GOOD LOSER. An athlete who is capable of making reporters believe he enjoyed being beaten.   *Jimmy Cannon*
— The thing we like to believe the other feller is.
                                                    Harry Ruby
GOOD OLD DAYS. When the prisoner, not the sentence, was suspended.   *Wall Street Journal*
GOOD SECRETARY. A stenographer who must think like a man, act like a lady, and work like a horse.   *Anon.*
GOOD SPEECH. Like a baby—easy to conceive but hard to deliver.   *Rep. Emanuel Celler*
GOOD TASTE. A definite lack of a sense of publicity.
                                                    Cecil Roberts

GOOD TIMES. When people who used to go around barefoot start complaining about the price of shoes.
Maurice Seitter

GOOSE. A low heavy bird which is most meat and feathers. Geese can't sing much on account of the dampness of the water. He ain't got no between-his-toes and he's got a little balloon in his stummick to keep him from sinking. Some geese when they are big has curls on their tails and is called ganders. Ganders don't have to sit and hatch, but just eat and loaf around and go swimming. If I was a goose, I'd rather be a gander.   *Anon., Jr.*

GORGONS. Three sisters that lived in the islands of the Hesperides somewhere in the Indian Ocean. They had long snakes for hair, tusks for teeth, and claws for nails, and they looked like women, only more horrible.   *Anon., Jr.*

GORILLA. The only other animal that picks its teeth.
Fact Digest
GORILLA WARFARE. When the sides get up to monkey tricks.
Anon., Jr.

GOSH DARN! A good goddamn.

GOSSAMER. "The nearest thing to nothing—and better in black."   *Macy's*

GOSSIP. Putting one and one together to make talk.
— A person who puts two and two together—whether they are or not.   *Mary McCoy*
— Sociologists on a mean and petty scale.   *Woodrow Wilson*
GOSSIP COLUMNIST. A man who makes many marital graves with little digs.   *Morton Thompson*

GOT. To sever with a knife, or that which is severed, i.e., "His a testy got current-biff."   *New Yorkese*

GOUNOD, CHARLES. A base soul who poured a sort of bathwater melody down the back of every woman he met; Margaret or Madeleine, it was all the same.
George Moore

GOURMAND. An adult who can eat almost as much as a small child. *Cynic's Cyclopaedia*

GOUT. Exterior, as "The kid is groan gout of his clothes." *New Yorkese*

GOVERNMENT. A system for keeping people in line—especially at windows.
— A group of men organized to sell protection to the inhabitants of a limited area at monopolistic prices. *Maxwell Anderson*
  GOVERNMENT CONTROL. The way to stop the wheels of progress—look what it did to the Pony Express!
  GOVERNMENT IN EXILE. A status quo in a vacuum.

GOVERNOR. A device attached to a state to keep it from going ahead very fast.
  LIEUTENANT GOVERNOR. A man who gets up every morning and inquires whether the Governor's any worse. *Will Rogers*

GRAFT. An illegal means of uniting trees to make money. *Anon., Jr.*

GRAMMAR. The science of putting language in its place.
— A book about the way people talk in books.

GRANDFATHER. An O.K. A.K.

GRANDMA. An old lady who keeps your mother from spanking you. *Anon. child*

GRANT, U. S. A man who had made up his mind to drive his head through a stone wall. *Anon. Union officer*

GRAPEFRUIT. Eyewash.

GRATITUDE. The cheapest interest on debt.
— Merely a secret hope of greater favors. *La Rochefoucauld*
— The most painful thing to bear, next to ingratitude. *Henry Ward Beecher*

GRAVE. The last resort.
  GRAVEYARD. Death's dormitory.

GRAVITATION. What, if there were none, we should fly away.
                                        Anon., Jr.

GRAVITY. The force that tells us why an apple does not go to
  heaven.   *Anon., Jr. (British Division)*
— A force that pulls down the corners of the mouth.
— A mysterious carriage of the body to conceal a defect of
  the mind.   *Laurence Sterne*

GRAY, THOMAS. A dull fellow. He was dull in a new way, and
  that made many people call him great.
                                   Dr. Samuel Johnson

GREAT DANE. A dog who has the house broke before he is.
                                      Fibber McGee

GREEK TRAGEDY. The sort of drama where one character says
  to another: "If you don't kill Mother, I will."
                                      Spyros Skouras

GREENHORN. One who arrived a day after you.

GREENWICH VILLAGE. Hell's kitchenette.   *College Humor*
  GREENWICH VILLAGE FLAT. A penthouse in the basement.
                                      Helen Morgan

GROAN. An expression of appreciation for the horrible.

GROOVE. A longer grave.

GROSS (Theatrical) net plus nut.
  GROSS DARKNESS. A kind of religious darkness, one hundred
    and forty-four times as dark as ordinary dark.
                             Anon., Jr. (British Division)

GRUNT. The great-great-great grandfather of "So what?"

GUFFY. The universal American beverage.   *New Yorkese*
  DOC GUFFY. Without cream.   *Ibid.*

GUILD. A wing-collar union.

GUILLOTINE. The only real cure for dandruff.

GUILT. The unfortunate circumstance that hangs people.
Robert Louis Stevenson
— A cat in a birdcage. *Preston Sturges**

GUITAR. A hillbilly harp. *Anon.*

GULCH. A dirty crack.

GUNPOWDER. Hasty ageing. *Scotch proverb*
— Insecticide for humans.
— A substance employed in marking the boundary lines of
nations. *Cynic's Cyclopaedia*

GURGLE. To gargle with pleasure.

GUSTO. A homemade relish.

GUTENBERG, JOHANNES. A man who cut himself a niche by
copying a Chink.

GUTTERS. The brooks of the city.

GUTTURAL. Gutter talk.

GUZZLE. To gargle with spirits.

H

H. Although much difference is often produced in the meaning of a word by the omission of the aspirate, there is sometimes a curious analogy between two words with and without the "h." For instance, with the "ear" one "hears," with an "axe" one "hacks," at the "edge" of a field there is a "hedge," the "hall" of the castle was for "all." On the other hand, "hair" is distinct from "air," "harrow" from "arrow," "helm" from "elm." "H" should still have its value in such words as "whither" and "where," which are the descendants of the Old English *hwidir* and *hwoer*, but the letter has been entirely dropped in "loaf" from *hlaf*, in "neck" from *hnecca*, and in "ring" from *hring*.

Basil Hargrave

H₂O. Hot water.

CO_2. Cold water. *Anon., Jr.*

HABEAS CORPUS. A phrase of the Great Plague meaning "Bring out your dead." *Anon., Jr. (British Division)*

HABITS. Iron shirts. *Yugoslavian proverb*
— First cobwebs, then cables. *Spanish proverb*

HACIENDA. A castle in Spain.

HACK. A writer who is making a living. *Leonard Neubauer**

HAGGARD. A portrait drawn with care.

HAGGLE. To attack the profit system.

HAIG & HAIG. Two Scotchmen who died many years ago but whose spirits live on and on.

HAIR. The only thing that will really prevent baldness.

Drew Berkowitz

97

HALLELUJAH. The capital of the Hawaiian Islands. *Anon., Jr.*

HALLUCINATION. A belief owned exclusively by one person.

HALO. A saintly spotlight.

HAM. An actor who makes a fat line seem greasy. *Anon.*

HAMLET. A place with only ten or twelve filling stations. *Ibid.*

HAND. A grappling hook attached to the human arm.
HANDBILL. A newspaper minus the lies.

HANDEL. The Thunderbolt. *Mozart*

HANDICAPPER. A guy who makes money breaking people.
Jimmy Cannon
HANG. To suspend indefinitely.
HANGING. The worst use man can be put to. *Henry Wotton*
HANGMAN. A jerk-of-all-trades.

HANGOVER. Something to occupy a head that wasn't used
the night before. *Howard W. Newton*
— Where the brew of the night meets the cold of the day.
Arizona *Kitty Kat*

HAPPINESS. The absence of pain. *Chinese saying*
— A delicate balance between what one is and what one has.
F. H. Denison
— The greatest cosmetic for beauty.
Lady Marguerite Blessington
— A peculiar feeling you acquire when you're too busy to be
miserable. *Anon.*
— Knowing that you do not necessarily require happiness.
William Saroyan
— Something to do, something to love, and something to hope
for. *Anon.*
— Something you used to have. *Lyon Mearson*
HAPPY. Having a scratch for every itch. *Ogden Nash*
HAPPY ENDING. One in which you lay down the book and
say: "Thank God *that's* over." *Morton Thompson*

HARA-KIRI. A Japanese apology.

HARD TIMES (Hollywood). A season during which it is very difficult for the studios to borrow money to make pictures the public won't go to see.   *Frank Morgan*

HARDY, THOMAS. A miscarriage of George Eliot.
                                         George Moore

HAREM. A community of women who subscribe to a circulating husband.
   HAREM SCAREM. The conduct of a man who can't afford a harem.

HARP. A nude piano.   \   *Tom O. Horgan*

HARRIDAN. A woman who has been seen better nights.

HASH HOUSE. The place where every good little soda mint tablet wants to go when it dies.   *Don Quinn**

HAT. An article worn by men to conceal the shape of their heads. (Compare BRASSIERE.)
   TOP HAT. A cylinder surmounting a vacuum.
                                    *Norman Reilly Raine**

HATCHET MAN. One who cuts Chinks for a living.
— We wanted Li Wing
      But we winged Willy Wong;
   A sad but excusable
      Slip of the Tong.   *Keith Preston*

HATRED (Class). What makes kids play hooky.

HAUTEUR. Nothing, with its nose in the air.

HAWAII. Florida with climate.   *Earl Wilson*

HE IS DRUNK. The future of "he drinks."   *Anon., Jr.*

HE-MAN. A cross between a crooner and a chest wig—the kind of cross that gets harder to bear every year.
                                    *Morton Thompson**

HEADLIGHTS. Lamps carried on automobiles to blind oncoming drivers.

HEALTH. The thing that makes you feel that now is the best time of the year. *Franklin P. Adams*
— What people are always drinking to before they fall down.
Four Hundred & Four

HEATHEN COUNTRY. One where payrolls are not carried in armored cars.

HEAVEN. The Coney Island of the Christian imagination.
Elbert Hubbard

HEAVENS! The curse of respectability.

HEAVYWEIGHT CHALLENGER. Any pug who weighs over 175 pounds and can prove he isn't dead. *Jimmy Cannon*

HECKLER. An impediment in speech.

HEEL. That slice of the loaf with the most crust.

HEGIRA. An eastern queen who invited the barbarians into the Empire. *Anon., Jr.*

HEIR. He who gets what's left.

HELICOPTER. An egg beater with ambition. *Skyways*

HELL. A place where there are no fans. *Arabian proverb*
— A place paved with women's tongues. *Abbé Guyon*
— A place filled with pretty women and no mirrors.
— God's penitentiary. *Rev. Charles Jaynes, Jr. (Age 7)*

HEN. An egg's way of making another egg. *Samuel Butler*
— A very nice animal. It is formed by other hens sitting on eggs. Ducks are brought up in the same way. *Anon., Jr.*

HENRY, O. de Maupassant in a swimming pool. *Jim Tully*

HENRY VIII. A great widower. *Anon., Jr. (British Division)*

HERBACEOUS BORDER. One who boards all the week and goes home on Saturdays and Sundays. *Anon., Jr.*

HEREDITY. The theory that we get our worst points from our ancestors.
— When a teen-age boy winds up with his mother's big brown eyes and his father's long yellow convertible.
— If your grandfather didn't have any children, then your father probably wouldn't have had any, and neither would you, probably.   *Anon., Jr.*
— Something that runs in the family, as, a nose.

HERMIT. A man without an automobile.

HERO. One who is afraid to run away.   *English proverb*
— A soldier lucky enough to be seen while doing his duty.
American officer
— An ordinary man who is brave five minutes longer.
Ralph Waldo Emerson
— A man who is famous today and will bore us tomorrow.
HEROISM. Not giving a damn before witnesses.

HERS. His.   *Ambrose Bierce, 1881*
HIS. Hers (today).

HIALEAH. French for "Hello, Suckers."   *Anon.*

HIATUS. Breath that wants seeing to.
Anon., Jr. (British Division)

HICCOUGH. An irrelevant remark.

HICK TOWN. A community where there is no place to go where you shouldn't be.   *Robert Quillen*
— One where, if you see a girl dining with a man old enough to be her father, he is.   *Anon.*
— One where even a haircut changes the whole appearance of the community.   *Kin Hubbard*
— A community proud of its traffic congestion.
Anon. collegiate

HIDEBOUND. Covered with the living skin of an ass.

HIGH HEELS. Heels invented by a woman who had been kissed on the forehead.   *Christopher Morley*

HIGHBROW. A fellow who can listen to the *William Tell Over-ture* without thinking of "The Lone Ranger." *Jack Perlis*
— A person educated beyond his intelligence.
Brander Matthews
— A person who can discuss sex and make you think he meant it all in a purely intellectual way. *College Humor*
— A man who has discovered something more interesting than women. *Russell Lynes*
— The kind of person who looks at a sausage and thinks of Picasso. *A. P. Herbert*
LOWBROW. The kind of person who looks at Picasso and thinks of baloney.

HIGHWAY. The space between billboards. *Anon. collegiate*
— The shortest distance between two detours.

HINTERLAND. The part of the country that's behind.

HIRED GIRLS. The principal exports of Sweden. *Anon., Jr.*

HISTORY. Man, his story.
— Dry gossip.
— Dry rot.
— A small thing to write about. *Hendrick W. Van Loon*
— A compound of poetry and philosophy.
Thomas Babington Macaulay
— Nothing more than legend and romance. *Thomas Wright*
— Petrified imagination. *Arthur "Bugs" Baer*
— Little more than a register of the crimes, follies, and mis-fortunes of mankind. *Gibbon*
— That terrible mill in which sawdust rejoins sawdust.
Dame Edith Sitwell
— A confused heap of facts. *Lord Chesterfield*
— A pack of tricks played upon the dead. *Voltaire*
— The crystallization of popular beliefs. *Donn Piatt*
— Something that repeats itself; historians repeat each other.
Philip Guedalla
— A lie agreed upon. *Anon.*
— Not so much a lie agreed upon as a waking dream.
F. Yates-Brown

— A narrative of designs which have failed, and hopes that have been disappointed. *Samuel Johnson*

HISTORICAL NOVEL. A book with a shapely wench on the jacket but no jacket on the shapely wench. *Earl Wilson*
HISTORIAN. An editor of yesterday's news.

HITCHHIKE. A long walk sitting down.

HITLER. A combination of initiative, perfidy, and political epilepsy. *Trotsky*
— An I, beer, noise, and threat specialist. *Don Quinn**
HITLERISM. Pathology in politics. *Walter Bartz*

HOARDING. Patting a dime on the head and wishing it would grow up.

HOBBY. Hard work you would be ashamed to do for a living. *Gilbert Norwood*
— Something you do in your spare time that bores all of your friends so much they don't come around any more, which gives you more spare time for your hobby.
— A particular thing you go goofy over in order to keep from going nuts over things in general. *Anon.*

HOCKEY. Mayhem on ice.

HOG. Twenty bushels of corn walking. *Chicago version*

HOGARTH. Author of many satirical works, including "The Rape's Progress." *Anon., Jr.*

HOLE. Nothing at all, but you can break your neck in it. *Austin O'Malley*

HOLIDAY. A day when father works twice as hard as he does at the office.

HOLLYWOOD. The place bad plays go when they die. *George Jean Nathan*
— The psychopathic ward of Art. *Douglas Churchill**
— The only asylum run by its inmates. *Grover Jones*

— The world's most beautiful set and the lousiest scenario.

Harry Hirschfield*

— A gold rush in dinner jackets. *Boris Morros*

— A western mining camp with service from the Ritz.

Walter Wanger

— The Klondike with Venetian blinds. *Harry Hirschfield**

— A warm Siberia. *Anon.*

— Six suburbs in search of a city. *Jimmy Gleason*

— The Athens of Los Angeles County. *Virginia Faulkner*

— The musical comedy version of Cedar Rapids.

— An emotional Detroit. *Lillian Gish*

— A town that has to be seen to be disbelieved.

— A place where a clerk in Schwab's asked Marlon Brando for his autograph. And then, a few minutes later, when Marlon asked this same clerk to cash a check for him, she asked him if he had any identification to prove who he was.

— A town where they place you under contract instead of observation. *Walter Winchell*

— A place where they pat you on the back to your face and kick you in the face to your back.

Dennis O'Keefe's press agent

— A place where they find out what you don't like—and then give you plenty of it. *Joe Frisco*

— The only place in the world where you can go to a formal dinner dressed for a picnic and feel thoroughly at ease.

William Gargan

— A place where they shoot too many pictures and not enough actors. *Walter Winchell*

— A place where everyone is a genius until he loses his job.

Erskine Johnson

— A sunny spot for shady people. *Anon.*

— Ten million dollars' worth of intricate and highly ingenious machinery, functioning elaborately to put skin on baloney.

George Jean Nathan

— A giant public privy with all those on the outside dying to get in and all those on the inside doing their damnedest to get out. *Elsie Dinsmore**

— A state of mind surrounded by Los Angeles.

Morton Thompson

— A place where the stars employ doubles to do all their dangerous jobs for them, excepting marriage. *Tom Jenk*

— The place where, if a guy's wife looks like a new woman, she probably is. *Roger Price*

— A place where behind every successful husband there's another woman. *Anon.*

— No place for a girl to find a husband, especially her own.

Denise Darcel

— No place for a professional comedian—there's too much amateur competition. *Fred Allen*

— The white folks' Harlem.

HOLLYWOOD BOULEVARD. The rue rue. *Morton Thompson*

HOLLYWOOD CORRESPONDENT. A visitor whose home town has a newspaper.

HOLLYWOOD GENTLEMAN. A guy who steps on his cigarette so it won't burn your rug. *Helen Forrest*

HOLY ROLLER. A jumping Jehoshaphat. *Kay Norton**

HOLY ROMAN EMPIRE. A country which was neither holy, Roman, nor an empire. *Voltaire*

HOME. A place to go when all the other joints are closed.

Anon.

— The place where, when you have to go there, they take you in. *Robert Frost*

— A place where you can scratch any place you itch.

Henry Ainsley

— A suit of clothes with a roof on it.

— An Englishman's castle while his wife is at the pictures.

Magazine Digest

— A place where part of the family waits until the others are through with the car. *Annapolis Log*

— Where you live with your loved ones. *Anon., Jr.*

HOUSE. A big mansion on a hill with plenty of trouble.

Ibid.

HOME COOKING. Where many a husband thinks his wife is.
Eddie Davis

HOME RUN. When de ball goes where de people isn't, den dat's good. *Elsa Martinelli*

HOMELINESS. The best guardian of a young girl's virtue.
Mme. de Genlis

HOMESICK. Craving the place you just escaped from.

HONEST. Undetected.
HONESTY. A golfer's chief handicap. *Maclean's*
— The best foreign policy. Mount Airy *Record-News*

HONEYMOON. The morning after the knot before.
Typo Graphic

HONOR. What a girl loses when she gains experience.
HONORABLE. Afflicted with an impediment in one's reach.
Ambrose Bierce

HOOD, THOMAS. A poet who always sang songs in his shirt. He was no madder than most poets.
Anon., Jr. (British Division)

HOOLIGAN. A polygon with seven sides. *Anon., Jr.*

HOPE. Dope. *Ogden Nash*
— Faith in charity.

HORIZON. A line where the earth and sky meet, but which disappears when you get there.
Anon., Jr. (British Division)

HOROSCOPE. A prognostication based on the belief that the date of your birth has a relationship with your life.
INSURANCE. A prognostication based on the belief that the date of your birth has a relationship with your death.

HORS DE COMBAT. A war horse. *Anon., Jr.*

HORS D'OEUVRE. A ham sandwich cut into forty pieces.
Jack Benny
— Out of work. *Anon., Jr.*

HORSE. Man's best friend until someone invented a machine that went faster.

    HORSE PLAYER. A guy who buys $200 worth of hope for 2 minutes for $2. *Eddy Howard*

    — A person who feels wretched on a Sunday for what he did on Saturday and is going to do on Monday. *Charles Degen*

    HORSE SENSE. A degree of wisdom that keeps one from betting on the races. *Foolish Dictionary*

    — That rare intelligence that keeps horses from betting on human beings. *Bob Burns*

    — An insult to a noble and useful animal. *Ludwig Lewisohn*

    — Stable thinking. *Texas chemistry student*

    HORSEMANSHIP. The ability to remain unconcerned and on a horse simultaneously.

HOSPITAL. The only place you can get into without having baggage. They don't hold the trunk like a hotel does . . . they just hold the body. *Will Rogers*

— A place where you go to be born. *Anon., Jr.*

    HOSPITAL ROOM. A place where friends of the patient go to talk to other friends of the patient. *Francis O. Walsh*

HOSTAGE. A lady who entertains visitors. *Anon., Jr.*

HOT-ROD. The old-fashioned sofa motorized. *Anon.*

HOTEL. An establishment where a guest often gives up good dollars for poor quarters. *Foolish Dictionary*

HOUSE. A hiding place from nature.

    HOUSE OF LORDS. The British Outer Mongolia for retired politicians. *Anthony Wedgwood Benn (Lord Stansgate)*

    VACANT HOUSE. An obsolete term.

    HOUSEBOAT. A domicile that enables its owner to live on his swimming pool.

    HOUSEWARMING. The last call for wedding presents. *June Provines*

    HOUSEWIFE. One who buys the potato salad herself.

HUBBARD, ELBERT. The P. T. Barnum of culture.   *Anon.*

HUG. Energy gone to waist.   *Anon.*

HULA. A series of bumps done sideways.   *Sherry Britton*

HUMAN. An automatic machine that would run perfectly if it did not have the power of judgment.
> HUMAN BEING. An ingenious assembly of portable plumbing.
> *Christopher Morley*
> HUMAN BEINGS. The only animals of which I am thoroughly and cravenly afraid.   *George Bernard Shaw*
> HUMAN NATURE. What makes you swear at the driver when you are a pedestrian and at the pedestrian when you're the driver.   *Bainbridge Mainsheet*
> HUMANS. The greatest of the earth's parasites.
> *Dr. Martin H. Fischer*

HUMILIATION. An emotion caused by suddenly shrinking to our normal proportions.   Fort Mifflin *Bulletin*
HUMILITY. The pride of the humble.

HUMOR. A kind of emotional chaos told calmly and quietly in retrospect.   *James Thurber*
HUMORIST. A comedian who doesn't tell dirty stories.
Gordon Currie
— An exhumerist.   *Milton Berle (who ought to know)*

HUNCH. What you call an idea that you're afraid is wrong.
Carter Dickson

HUNGER. The positive form of appetite.
— An S O S from the stomach.
— The mother of Fascism.   *Joseph Ferdinand Gould*

HUSBAND. The critic on the hearth.
— A man who has chased a woman until she has caught him.
El Paso *Times*
— One who has several small mouths to feed and one big one to listen to.   *Vince Montemora*
— Person who expects his wife to be perfect and to understand why he isn't.   *Anon.*

— Something no respectable family should be without.

Fred Allen

— What's left of a sweetheart after the nerve has been killed.

Abbott & Costello*

HUSBAND HUNTING. The only sport in which the animal that gets caught has to buy a license.   *Cy N. Peace*

HUSSY. An equine, as in "Giddy-yap, hussy."   *New Yorkese*

HUZZAH. The hussar's hurrah.

HYDRAULICS. The writing in Ancient Egypt.   *Anon., Jr.*

HYMEN. The god of Chaos.   *Anon., Jr.*

HYPOCHONDRIA. The malady that malingers on.
   HYPOCHONDRIAC. A person who calls a doctor when he wants an audience.   Putnam County *News*
   — A person with a sham pain.
   — A guy who can't leave being well enough alone.
   — One who insists on being buried next to a doctor.

Steve Lawrence

HYPOCRISY. The prevailing religion of England.   *Anon., Jr.*
   — The homage which vice pays virtue. *La Rochefoucauld*
HYPOCRITE. One who thinks that she is what she isn't when she ain't.   *Kate Douglas Wiggin*

HYPOTHESIS. Hippo, horse; thesis, placing. Putting something on a horse.   *Anon., Jr. (British Division)*

HYSTERICS. Letters in sloping type.   *Anon., Jr.*

I

I.O.U. A type of paper wait. *Skyscrapers*

IBEX. Where you look at the back of the book to find out anything you want. *Anon., Jr.*

IBID. A prolific writer of quotations (no relation to Ovid or Avid).
— A famous Latin poet. *Ibid.*

ICE. An example of hard water. *Anon., Jr.*
   ICE COOL. The institution of learning which stands midway between grammar school and college. *Charlestonese*
   ICEBERG. A permanent wave. *Mickey Mouse*

ICICLE. A congealed weapon.
— A drip caught in a draft. *Anon.*
— A stiff piece of water. *Fred Allen*

ICONS. What you fatten pigs on under oak trees. *Anon., Jr.*

IDEAL GUEST. One who stays at home. *Edgar Watson Howe*

IDEAL HUSBAND. One who feels in his pockets every time he passes a mailbox. *Bedside Examiner*

IDEAL WIFE. Any woman who has an ideal husband.
Booth Tarkington

IDEALIST. A man who is for anything as long as it doesn't hurt business. *Anon.*

IDEAS. Funny little things that won't work unless you do.
Columbia Record

IDIOT. A man who takes no part in public affairs.
Original meaning
— A man who takes part in public affairs. *Modern meaning*
   IDIOTIC. Easily pleased.

IDLENESS. The mother of mischief. *Col. Thomas H. Perkins*
— The art of being a vegetable.

IDOL. A feat of clay.

IGNORAMUS. Someone who doesn't know something that you
learned yesterday. *Anon.*

IGNORANCE. A by-product of education.
— The art of relying on experts.

ILLEGAL. A sick bird.

ILLITERATE CHILD. One whose parents are not married.
Anon., Jr.

IMAGINATION. The one weapon in the war against reality.
Jules de Gaultier
— What puts men in asylums unless they are crazy enough
to put it down on paper or canvas.
— What makes some politicians think they are statesmen.
Roberta Tennes
— The thing which prevents us from being as happy in the
arms of a chambermaid as in the arms of a duchess.
Dr. Samuel Johnson
— Imagination is something not regulated by fate;
It's what a woman sits with when her hubby stays out late.
Jack Allis

IMBECILE. One who is satisfied with the brains he is born
with.
— A germ floating around in the air which anybody is liable
to catch. *Anon., Jr.*

IMITATION. The sincerest form of insult. *Elbert Hubbard*
— The sincerest form of envy. *Anon.*
— The sincerest form of radio. *Fred Allen*
— The sincerest form of monkey business.
IMITATOR. A stand-in for a stand-out. *Anon.*

IMMORTALITY. An actor's belief in curtain calls.

IMMUNITY (Natural). Being able to catch a disease without the aid of a physician. *Anon., Jr.*

IMPALED. Getting the point.

IMPATIENCE. The past tense of amiability.
— Waiting in a hurry. *Anon., Jr.*

IMPERIALISM. International kleptomania.
Cynic's Cyclopaedia

IMPLEMENT (Bureaucratese). What you do to carry out a decision, policy, or program when you are doing nothing. *Russell Baker*

IMPORTANT ANNOUNCEMENT (Advertising). Euphemism for a sales talk read into forty million deserted living rooms while folks out in Televisionland put fresh heads on beer. *Russell Baker*

IMPORTS. Ports very far inland. *Anon., Jr. (British Division)*

IMPOTENT. Heir-minded but not heir-conditioned. *Stewart Edward White*

IMPRESARIO. A promoter with an opera cape.

IMPROPRIETY. The soul of wit. *W. Somerset Maugham*

INCENSE. A wishful stink.

INCENTIVE. The possibility of getting more money than you can earn.

INCINERATOR. A person who hints bad things instead of coming right out and telling you. *Anon., Jr.*

INCOGNITO. A royal alias.

INCOME. Something that you can't live without or within. *Harry B. Behrmann*

INCOME-TAX EXPERT. Someone whose fee is the amount he saves you in making out your tax. *Dan Bennett*

INCOMPATIBILITY. The greatest common divisor.

INCONSISTENCY. To avoid the rain by standing under the
spout.   *Anon.*

INCONSPICUOUS. Prominently timid.

INDEMNITY. An ill-gotten gain.

INDIAN RESERVATION. The home of the brave.
— A mile of land for every five square Indians.   *Anon., Jr.*
   INDIANS. Natives who travel in birchbark canoes on little
   streams of water that they make themselves.   *Anon., Jr.*

INDIGESTION. A falling out between the head and the stomach.

INDISCRETION. The better part of valor.   *Samuel Butler*

INDIVIDUAL. One piece of people.   *Anon., Jr.*

INERTIA. The ability to rest.   *Anon., Jr.*

INFANT. A tender human succulent.
— A disturber of the peace.   *Foolish Dictionary*
   INFANT PRODIGY. A small child with highly imaginative
   parents.   *R. H. Creese*

INFERIORITY COMPLEX. The feeling that sweeps over a notori-
ous hold-up man when he gets his check in a night club.
                                                Temple Owl

INFIDEL. One who commits infidelity.
— A Christian in Constantinople.   *Ambrose Bierce*

INFINITY. A floorless room without walls or ceiling.
                                                Sour Owl
— The living end.   *Anon.*

INFLATION. Air in the dough.
— A drop in the buck.   *Pueblo Pete*
— Being broke with a lot of money in your pocket.
                                Industrial Press Service

— When you never had it so good or parted with it so fast.

Max Hess

— When one can live as cheaply as two. *Anon.*

— When dollars to doughnuts becomes an even-money bet.

INFLUENCE. A power you think you have until you try to use it. *Anon.*

INGENUE. An actress who gets billing by cooing.

INGENUITY. Genius in trifles. *Anon.*

INGRATE. A man who bites the hand that feeds him—and then complains of indigestion. *Harry Hirshfield**

INJECTION. A shout or scream raised by a person too surprised or frightened to make a sentence with his thoughts. It is not quite a human language. The lower animals say nothing else but injections. Accordingly ill-natured and cross people by their injections come very near to beasts.

Anon., Jr. (British Division)

INJUSTICE. Relatively easy to bear; what stings is justice.

H. L. Mencken

INNOCENCE. A circumstance of victims.
INNOCENT. Unproven.

INQUISITION. A play presented at the court of Ferdinand and Isabella. *Anon., Jr.*

INSANE ASYLUM. A bug bin. *Anon.*

INSANITY. To art what garlic is to salad.

Augustus Saint-Gaudens

INSIDE DOPE. Anything a dope on the outside will believe.

Millard Faught & Laurence Hammond

INSPIRATION. A force that poets have invented to give themselves importance. *Jean Anouilh*

INSTALLMENT BUYING. A method invented to make the months seem shorter.

INSTANT. A breath-taking division of time.

INSURANCE. A guarantee that, no matter how many necessities a person had to forgo all through life, death was something to which he could look forward.   *Fred Allen*
— Paying for catastrophe on the installment plan.
   UNEMPLOYMENT INSURANCE. Half a loaf.

INTEGRITY. The virtue of being good without being watched.

INTELLIGENCE. Horse sense in people.
   INTELLIGENTSIA. People who read each other's books.

INTERCOMMUNICATION SYSTEM. Something that can be shut off when you want to hear something.   *Don Quinn°*

INTERIOR DECORATOR. A man who does things to your house he wouldn't dream of doing to his own.   *Herb Shriner*

INTERN. A doctor with an amateur license.

INTERPRETER. A ventriloquist using two dummies.

INTERVALS. What most people work at.   *Anon.*

INTERVENE. To spread burning oil on troubled waters.

INTIMACY. The first step toward parenthood.

INTOXICATION. A temporary madness.   *Pythagoras*
— A cure for diphtheria.   *Anon., Jr.*

INTUITION. The gift which enables a woman to arrive instantly at an infallible and irrevocable decision without the aid of reason, judgment, or discussion.   *Corsair*
— Suspicion in skirts.   *Anon.*
— Something that tells you to go ahead and do the right thing after you considered doing the wrong thing and decided it wasn't worth the risk.

INVENTOR. A man with wheels in his head.

INVESTOR. A man who plays the horses on a merry-go-round.
— A speculator who hangs on when the price doesn't go up.
Charles E. Mitchell

IRELAND. A country in which the probable never happens and the impossible always does. *John Mahaffy*

IRISH. The Texans of Europe.
— The Puerto Ricans of the British Isles. *Anon.*
IRISH BULL. A male animal that is always pregnant.
John Mahaffy
— A horse of another color. *Anon.*

IRONY. An insult conveyed in the form of a compliment.
Anon.

IRRIGATION. Through the Alimentary Canal with Rod and Gun. *Frank Scully*

IRRITANT. A woman.

ISM. Something that has to be appreciated to be seen.

ISOLATIONIST. A man turned turtle.
— An advocate of spite fences on an international scale.
— One who wouldn't even touch a 10-foot Pole.

ISOSCELES. A Greek dramatist. *Anon., Jr.*

IT. To partake of food. *New Yorkese*

ITALY. A great prison where children are taught to adore their chains and to pity those who are free.
Lauro de Bosis, 1925

J

JACKSON, ANDREW. The most American of Americans—an embodied Declaration of Independence—the 4th of July incarnate. *James Parton*

JADE. A semiprecious stone or a semiprecious woman.
Oliver Herford

JAIL. Room and board for the worst members of a community, paid for by the rest.

JAMES, HENRY. An author who wrote fiction as if it were a painful duty. *Oscar Wilde*

JANITOR. One of the main causes of dust. *Anon., Jr.*

JANUARY. The beginning of a disappointment. *Bill Manville*

JAP. A perturbed Chinaman. *Charles Fort*

JAZZ. An appeal to the emotions by an attack on the nerves.
— Music that will endure as long as people hear it through their feet instead of their brains. *John Philip Sousa*
— Music invented by demons for the torture of imbeciles.
Henry Van Dyke

JEALOUSY. The friendship one woman has for another.
The Arcadians
— A way to get rid of everything you're afraid of losing.

JEEP. A vehicle which, if it were struck by lightning, the lightning would be towed away for repair. *Anon.*

JEHOVAH. The most fascinating character in all fiction.
Oliver Herford

JELL. Not fierce, i.e., "Ladies and jell men." *New Yorkese*

JEWELRY. Something people use in order to make out that they're better than other people. *Hugh Roy Cullen*
— A woman's best friend. *Edna Ferber*

JEW'S-HARP. An unmusical instrument played by holding it fast with the teeth and trying to brush it away with the fingers. *Ambrose Bierce*

JIGSAWS. What the people of Japan ride about in. *Anon., Jr.*

JIMMY. A small lever used by a felon to pry his way into jail.

JITTERBUG. A person vaccinated with a riveting machine.
Ben Bernie
JITTERBUGGING. Twerpsichore. *Don Quinn**

JOAN OF ARC. Noah's wife. *Anon., Jr. (British Division)*

JOHN BIRCH SOCIETY. That pathetic manifestation of organized apoplexy. *Edward P. Morgan*

JOHNSON, DR. SAMUEL. That pompous, disagreeable old man who differs from other forgotten and unread writers in that his biographer was a genius. *Vincent Sheean*

JOINT ACCOUNT. An account where one person does the depositing and the other the withdrawing. *Anon.*

JOURNALISM. Literature in a hurry. *Matthew Arnold*
— The infinite capacity for making pain.
JOURNALIST. A newspaperman out of a job. *Elbert Hubbard*
— A near-sighted historian.

JOY. A fruit that Americans eat green. *Amando Zegri*

JOYCE, JAMES. The greatest punster who ever lived.
Clifton Fadiman

JUDGE. A man who seeks the truth and occasionally finds it, but doesn't know what to do about it. *Anon.*
— A referee between two other lawyers.

— A law student who marks his own examination papers.
                                                    H. L. Mencken
— A lawyer who knew a governor.   *Judge Mahoney*

JUJITSU. The practical demonstration that there are no irresistible forces and no immovable bodies.

JURY. A group of twelve people of average ignorance, chosen to decide who has the best lawyer.
— A body of citizens who will try anyone once.
     JUROR. A man picked from a poll list who hasn't enough political pull to get off a jury.
                                     Judge Robert Stewart Sutliffe

JUSTICE. A kind of compact not to harm or be harmed.
                                                          Epicurus
— A system of revenge wherein the State imitates the criminal.   *Elbert Hubbard*
— A decision in your favor.   *Harry Kaufman**

JUVENILE DELINQUENT. A kid who starts acting like his parents.   *Snag Werris*

K

K. I once tried to elevate myself status-wise. Likewise-wise I demoted myself alphabetically-wise from a "K" to an "R." This strained exercise, like the preceding sentences, resulted in utter confusion. Let me explain.

A few decades ago I was a successful theatrical press agent supplying loud and cackling noises while the playwrights I represented produced the golden eggs. My name and effusions appeared in various newspaper columns and some of my stories were published in *The New Yorker*. My income was modest but, if I may be immodest, I was known in the purlieus of Broadway.

Eventually I left New York to become a writer of motion pictures. My income increased but my standing in Celluloidia was such that when my name was mentioned the usual response, with rising inflection, was "Who?"

Hollywood offered very little in the way of diversion. There were occasional Broadway plays, its cast and scenery frayed and tattered from a long road tour. There were concerts and prize fights and wrestling and movies and movies and movies.

Whenever I attended a concert or a prize fight or a play I would get my ticket from a speculator. Although I paid a premium, somehow I found myself sitting in the fifteenth row, never in front. Reluctantly I faced the fact that as far as Hollywood was concerned, I was a distinguished nonentity.

Now, about my demotion from a "K" to an "R." There was a particular prize fight I wanted to see and it occurred to me that if I could impress Lou Frenkel, the speculator, perhaps I would be propelled forward in the area of the ringside seats. I thought of using the name of a film star but if Frenkel detected the fraud because of an acute ear, I would find myself behind a post.

It was then that my eyes were captured by a headline in the *Hollywood Reporter,* a trade paper. JOHN J. RASKOB TO BUY PARAMOUNT it proclaimed. Surely, I reflected, here was a prominent financier, the mention of whose name would win solicitous attention. I promptly called up Frenkel, asked for a ticket for the fights and when he asked my name, I said, "Raskob." "How do you spell it?" he inquired. This was a bit of a setback but I thought I'd spell it first and later explain the Raskob position and prominence. "R-a-s-k-o-b," I enunciated, but the moment I said "k-o-b" I automatically completed the rest of my name and added "e-r." And so I picked up one ticket in the name of Raskober and saw the fights from the fifteenth row.

I should have favored someone with a name beginning with a "K" like mine. Kubelsky, for instance. Everybody in Hollywood knows Jack Benny.   *Arthur Kober**

K-RATION. War fare.   *Frank W. Lewis*

KAFFIRS. A very savage African race. In time of war they beat their tum-tums and can be heard for many miles around.   *Anon., Jr.*

KANGAROO. A pogo stick with a pouch.   *Anon.*
— An animal that carries its brood in a snood.
                                        Harry McNaughton

KEEPER. Only a poacher turned outside in, and a poacher a keeper turned inside out.   *Charles Kingsley*

KENNY, NICK. Maxie Rosenbloom with a typewriter.
                                        Jack E. Leonard

KENTUCKY. Where the hoot owls howl in the daytime.
                                        Jess Stuart

KEYHOLE. An aperture which enables a door to be made fast and those within to be made loose.

KIBITZER. A guy who picks up a girl on another fellow's whistle.   *Anon.*
— The unmarried Siamese twin. *Anon. married Siamese twin*

KICKSY-WICKSY. A wife.   *Shakespeare*

KILTS. An article of dress first worn by a Scotchman who won a skirt in a raffle.

KIN. An affliction of the blood.

KINDRED. Fear that relatives are coming to stay.
                                                   Wes Lawrence

KING. A very ordinary kind of man who has to live in a very extraordinary kind of way that sometimes seems to have little sense to it.   *King George V*
— An official who today has become a vermiform appendix: useless when quiet; when obtrusive, in danger of removal.
                                                   Austin O'Malley
— A highly paid model for a postage stamp.   *Anon.*
EX-KING. One who has come in out of the reign.

KISS. A rosy dot over the i of loving.   *Cyrano*
— A thing of use to no one, but prized by two.   *Anon.*
— That which you cannot give without taking, and cannot take without giving.   *Anon.*
— A contraction of the mouth due to an enlargement of the heart.   *Anon.*
— A course of procedure, cunningly devised for the mutual stoppage of speech at a moment when words are superfluous.   *Oliver Herford*
— If you are ever in doubt as to whether or not you should kiss a pretty girl, always give her the benefit of the doubt.
                                                   Thomas Carlyle
— The anatomical juxtaposition of two orbicularis oris muscles in a state of contraction.   *Anon.*
— A vigorous exchange of saliva.   *Capt. Van Velsor,*
          physical educator, Rensselaer Polytechnic Institute
KISSING. Lip service to love.
— Nose-rubbing among the civilized.

KITCHENETTE. A narrow aisle that runs between a gas stove and a can of tomatoes.   *Bob Burns*

KLEPTOMANIA. Petty theft by a grand person.

    KLEPTOMANIAC. A person who suffers from fits of abstraction. *Anon.*

    — A person who helps himself because he can't help himself. *Henry Morgan*

    — A rich thief. *Ambrose Bierce*

KNIGHTHOOD. Honor bestowed by a king to change the subject.

KNITTING. An exercise that gives women something to think about when they are talking. *Anon.*

KNOWLEDGE. An arboriform stratification of guesses. *Anon.*

KODAK. The Bible of the Mohammedans. *Anon., Jr.*

KU KLUX KLAN. An organization of idealists who find it best to hide their faces.

L

LABOR. A force by which gold is pumped from one pocket into another.
— The curse of the working class.
  LABORER. A man who goes to work before 9 A.M.

LACROSSE. Running 20 miles to hit somebody over the head with a snowshoe. *College Humor*

LADY. A woman who always remembers others, and never forgets herself. *Charles Dana Gibson*
— A woman who can pull up a shoulder strap without going through the motions of a small boy scooping his new hat out of the mud. *Anon. collegiate*
  LADY IN WAITING. The feminine of bachelor. *Anon., Jr.*
  LADIES. The opposite of "Exit." *Ibid.*

LAISSEZ FAIRE. The theory that if each acts like a vulture, all will end as doves. *Leo C. Rosten*

LAND BARON. A ground hog.

LANGUAGE. A system of signs, grunts and hisses.
— The refined use of the tongue for the expression of opinion.
  FIGURATIVE LANGUAGE. When you mean a rooster and say chandelier. *Anon., Jr.*

LAPEL. The only tangible thing to be grasped in an argument.

LAPSE. What you get when you sit down. *Anon.*

LATITUDE. What tells you how hot you are: longitude, how cold you are. *Anon., Jr. (British Division)*

124

LAUGH. A smile that burst. *John E. Donovan*
LAUGHTER. An exercise in which men show their wit and women their teeth.
— The sensation of feeling good all over and showing it principally in one spot. *Josh Billings*

LAUNDRY. A place where they turn pajamas into negligee.
College Humor
— A receiver of stolen towels.

LAW. A machine to which men are sent to be laundered.
— The bandage over the eyes of Justice.
— A net to catch the fly and let the hawk go free.
Spanish proverb
— The errors that have the most followers.
— The lesser of two evils.
— The proof of the infallibility of ignorance. *Elbert Hubbard*
LAWSUIT. A method of collecting half the debt by compelling twice the payment.
LAWYER. A man you hire when you've murdered somebody and want it explained to the jury in the best possible light. *Frauds*
— A liar with a permit to practice.
— A learned gentleman who rescues your estate from your enemies and keeps it to himself. *Lord Brougham*
— Where there is a rift in the lute, the business of the lawyer is to widen the rift and gather the loot.
Arthur Garfield Hays
LAWYERS. Men who hire out their words and anger.
Martial, A.D. 20–102
— The trouble with law and government. *Clarence Darrow*
WASHINGTON LAWYER. A lobbyist with a degree.

LAWRENCE, T. E. An adventurer with a genius for backing into the limelight. *Lowell Thomas*

LAXITY. A cure for constipation. *Anon., Jr.*

LAYMAN. A citrus fruit. *New Yorkese*

LAZINESS. A bodily affliction which mostly the young indulge in, and only the old can afford. *Cynic's Cyclopaedia*

LEADER. The wave pushed ahead by the ship. *Tolstoy*

LEARNING. Like rowing upstream; not to advance is to drop back. *Chinese proverb*

LECHER. One who collects lechings. *Anon.*

LECTURE. The process by which the notes of the professor become the notes of the students without passing through the minds of either. *Professor Rathbun, Stanford*
LECTURER. One who makes talk money.
— A vocal acrobat.
— One with his hand in your pocket, his tongue in your ear, and his faith in your patience. *Ambrose Bierce*
LECTURERS. Traveling men who express themselves and collect. *Shannon Fife*

LEEK. The poor man's asparagus. *Anon. Frenchman*

LEFTIST. A liberal who just left.

LEGEND. Gossip down the ages.

LEGS. Things that if you ain't got two pretty good ones, you can't get to first base, and neither can your sister.
The Terminal Beacon

LEISURE. Time given the worker to play and the player to work.
— The opiate of the masses. *Malcolm Muggeridge*

LEOPARD. A dotted lion.

LETTER. A conversation between the absent and the present.
Wilhelm von Humboldt
LETTER WRITING. A most delightful way of wasting time.
John Morley
LETTRES DE CACHET. Perfumed letters. *Anon., Jr.*

LEVANT, OSCAR. The homely George Jessel. *Edith Gwynn*

LEVITY. The soul of wit. *Eli Perkins*

LEWIS, JOE E. The only man in the country with an honorary liquor license. *Jack E. Leonard*

LEWIS, SINCLAIR. A bashful cyclone. *Anon.*

LEXICOGRAPHER. The navvy of scholarship, carrying his head backward and forward from one learned library to another.
Osbert Burdett
— A bounder of words.
— A harmless drudge. *Dr. Samuel Johnson*

LIAR. One who tells the truth about something that never happened; hence a poet, a preacher, or a politician.
Elbert Hubbard
— A person who disagrees with President Roosevelt.
Abe Martin, 1907
— A bad adjective for boy. *Siamese student of English*

LIBERAL. A radical with a wife and child. *Anon.*
— A man who has just changed his mind. *Morton Thompson*
— Anyone whose ideas coincide with yours. *Russell Baker*

LIBERTY. Being free from the things we don't like in order to be slaves to the things we do like. *Anon.*
— Always dangerous, but it is the safest thing we have.
Harry Emerson Fosdick
— The right to elect people to make restrictions for you.
Dublin *Opinion*
— Patrick Henry's first choice.
— A bourgeois dream. *Lenin*
— Something you take with a lady. *Rupert Hughes*

LIBRARY. A room fraught with books and people.
Fred Allen
— A place where lies are buried.
   CIRCULATING LIBRARY. A collection of 15,000 mystery novels and 36 other books. *Anon.*

LIBRETTO. An Italian author. *Anon., Jr.*

LIE. A very poor substitute for the truth but the only one discovered up to date. *Foolish Dictionary*

LIEUTENANT COMMANDER. A lieutenant's wife. Calgary *Albertan*

LIFE. Trouble. *E. B. White*
— A breathing spell.
— A sentence that begins and ends with a yawn.
— The one incurable disease.
— The original do-it-yourself project.
— Nothing but buttoning and unbuttoning. *Lord Rosebery*
— A fortress. *Napoleon*
— A fairy tale. *Hans Christian Andersen*
— A jest. *John Gay*
— A ladder. *Sir Richard Burton*
— A tragedy. *Jonathan Swift*
— A flame. *George Bernard Shaw*
— A shuttle. *Shakespeare*
— A one-way street.
— A dream. *La Beaumelle*
— A state of warfare. *Seneca*
— A diary in which every man means to write one story, and writes another. *Sir James M. Barrie*
— Sobs, sniffles, and smiles, with sniffles predominating. *O. Henry*
— A carnival. *Souvestre*
— Not a spectacle or a feast; a predicament. *George Santayana*
— A tale told by an idiot. *Shakespeare*
— One long dirty trick. *Thorne Smith*
— A longish doze, interrupted by fits and starts of bewildered semialertness. *Clifton Fadiman*
— A sentence that man has to serve for the crime of being born. *Calderón*
— The flight of a sparrow (who thinks he is an eagle) from Muncie to Kokomo. *Yellow Crab*

— A vapour that appeareth for a little time then vanisheth away. *The Bible*

— A punishment for transgressions committed under an earlier form of being. *Hindu saying*

— A tale told in an idiom, full of unsoundness and fury, signifying nonism. *James Thurber*

— Ten per cent what you make it and 90 per cent how you take it. *Irving Berlin*

— An artichoke—you have to go through so much to get so little. *Tad*

— A span of time of which the first half is ruined by our parents and the second half by our children.
The Phoenix Flame

— Playing a violin solo in public and learning the instrument as one goes on. *Bulwer-Lytton*

— One long process of getting tired. *Samuel Butler*

— From diapers to dignity to decomposition. *Don Herold*

— A predicament which precedes death. *Thoreau*

— Just one stop sign after another. *Shell Oil Company*

— An experiment being conducted on one of the minor planets.

LIFETIME. A tick in an eternity.

CITY LIFE. Millions of people being lonesome together.
Thoreau

LIFE INSURANCE. An investment in disaster.
Mort & E. A. Gilbert

— Providing for the widows and orphans—of the officers and directors. *Harry Thompson*

LIGHT OPERA. A very simple formula—whatever isn't worth saying you sing. *Beaumarchais*

LIGHTNING. The awful autograph of God. *J. Millet*

LIMERICK. A witty ditty.

LINCOLN, ABRAHAM. Cinderella in prairie boots.
H. L. Mencken

— That mystic mingling of star and clod.
Congressman Fred Landis

LINGERIE. Underwear with lace on it.

LIONIZE. To treat a man like the king of beasts.

LIPSTICK. A device to make every kiss tell.

LIPTON. The capital of Ceylon. *Anon., Jr.*

LIQUOR. Instant courage. *Robert Sylvester*
— Totter Sauce.

LISP. To call a spade a thpade. *Oliver Herford*

LITERARY COLLABORATION. Togetherness with hives.
Robert Fontaine

LITERATURE. Only what people would say to each other if
they had the chance. *Christopher Morley*
— The orchestration of platitudes. *Thornton Wilder*

LITIGATION. A machine into which you go as a pig and come
out a sausage. *Ambrose Bierce*

LITRE. A nest of young puppies. *Anon., Jr.*

LITTER. The result of literary efforts.
Mrs. Leonard L. Levinson

LIVERY. The means whereby masters prevent themselves from
being taken for their servants. *Cynic's Cyclopaedia*

THE LIVING. The dead on holiday. *Maeterlinck*

LOAFER. A fellow who is trying to make both week ends
meet. *Anon.*

LOBBYIST. A man who is paid to tell congressmen how to vote.

LOBSTER. The Doris Day of the crab kingdom.

LOCK. A device to keep your neeboors honest.
Scottish proverb

LODGE. Not small. *New Yorkese*
— An association of men who love each other because it's
good for business. *Leonard Neubauer*°
LODGER. One who lives in and eats out.

LOGROLLING. An aye for an aye.

LONDON. A foggy Philadelphia.
— The metropolis New York thinks it is.
   LONDON CAB. An English gondola.   *Lord Beaconsfield*

LORGNETTE. A dirty look on a stick.   *Don Quinn**

LOS ANGELES. A sunny Des Moines.   *Anon.*
— Pittsburgh with oranges.
— The Ellis Island of the arts.   *Anon.*

LOTTERY. A tax on fools.   *Henry Fielding*

LOUDSPEAKER. A congressman.   *Cynic's Cyclopaedia*

LOVE. The art of assisting nature.   *Dr. Lallemand*
— Ownership.   *Henry Ward Beecher*
— A disease of the nymph glands.   *C. Julian**
— A kind of warfare.   *Ovid*
— A temporary insanity curable by marriage.
   Ambrose Bierce
— Sentimental measles.   *Charles Kingsley*
— An itch around the heart that you can't scratch.
   College Humor
— The dirty trick nature played on us to achieve the con-
tinuation of the species.   *W. Somerset Maugham*
— Love is like a dizziness; it winna let a puir body gang
about his business.   *James Hogg*
— A fire. But whether it is going to warm your hearth or
burn down the house, you can never tell.
   Strand (England)
— The union of a want and a sentiment.   *Balzac*
— A season pass on the shuttle between heaven and hell.
   Don Dickerman

— A compact with sorrow.
— A hot chili pepper—you know it's going to make you cry,
and still you go right ahead and eat it.
— The sire, dam, nurse, and seed
   Of all that air, earth, waters breed.
   Phineas Fletcher (1582–1650)

— A gross exaggeration of the difference between one person and everybody else. *George Bernard Shaw*

— A combination of sex and sentiment. *André Maurois*

— The triumph of imagination over intelligence.

H. L. Mencken

— Like a radiator—keeps you warm, even when you know it's only hot air. *Jerry Warren*

— A feeling that has the power of making you believe what you would normally treat with the deepest suspicion.

Marivau

— The effort a man makes to be satisfied with only one woman. *Paul Géraldy*

— A power too strong to be overcome by anything but flight.

Cervantes

— Propaganda for propagation.

— The companion of blindness. *Arabian proverb*

— Love is blind; that is why he always proceeds by the sense of touch. *French proverb*

— An ocean of emotion entirely surrounded by expenses.

Lord Dewar

— An ocean of emotion complete with gulls and buoys.

Granada *Review*

— The star that men look up to as they walk along. (MARRIAGE is the coal-hole they fall into.) *Anon.*

— A wonderful thing which is highly desirable in marriage.

Rupert Hughes

— The torrent that one checks by digging a bed for it.

Commerson

— One game never postponed on account of darkness.

The Houghton Line

— What makes the world go 'round—usually when it should be asleep. *H. C. Diefenbach*

— The need to escape from oneself. *Baudelaire*

— A magic that makes red hair "golden," white hair "silver," and no hair "a noble brow." *Anon.*

— A mutual misunderstanding. *Oscar Wilde*

— A mutual admiration society consisting of but two members. Of these, the one whose love is less intense will become president. *Joseph Mayer*

— Like a poached egg, at first it is very beautiful, and then when you mess around with it, it's all over the place.
Ish Kabibble

— "Love in a hut, with water and a crust,
Is—Love, forgive us!—cinders, ashes, dust." *John Keats*

— Something the minister throws in with "honor" and "obey."
Harry Hirshfield°

— Like the measles, all the worse when it comes late in life.
· *Lord Byron*

— The tenth word in a telegram. *Western Union*

— The most fun you can have without laughing. *Anon.*

— A nicer word. *Harry Kaufman°*

FIRST LOVE. A little foolishness and a lot of curiosity.
George Bernard Shaw

LOVE AT FIRST SIGHT. One of the greatest labor-saving devices the world has ever seen. *Josh Billings*

LOVE NEST. An exhibition of etchings. *Don Quinn°*

LOVE SONG. A caress set to music. *Sigmund Romberg*

LOVE TRIANGLE. Bisexing a two-faced figure, resulting in a wrecktangle. *Anon.*

PLATONIC LOVE. The gun you didn't know was loaded.
Anon.

TRUE LOVE. Friendship set on fire. *Jeremy Taylor*

LOW NECKLINE. Something you can approve of and look down on at the same time. *Winnie Garrett*

LUCIDITY. A niche in a nightmare.

LUCIFER. The inventor of the power dive.

LUMBAGO. A mineral used in making lead pencils. *Anon., Jr.*

LUNATIC ASYLUM. The place where optimism most flourishes.
Havelock Ellis

LUNCH COUNTER. A filling station for humans.

LUTHER, MARTIN. A man who died a horrible death. He was
excommunicated by a bull.   *Anon., Jr.*

LUXURY. A condition in which one has everything others
could wish for.

LYING. Fearing a fact.

LYNCHING. A double execution by a mob, one of the victims
being justice.
— Trial by fury.   *Newsweek*

LYRIC. Something written to be sung by a liar.   *Anon., Jr.*

LXXX. Love and kisses.   *Anon., Jr.*

M

M.D. Mentally deficient. *Anon., Jr.*

MACAULAY, THOMAS BABINGTON. A book in breeches. He has occasional flashes of silence that make his conversation perfectly delightful. *Sydney Smith*

MACDONALD, RAMSAY. A sheep in sheep's clothing.
Ernest Bevin

MADISON AVENUE. A defenseless abstraction that can be safely blamed for whatever you think is wrong with modern life, government, philosophy, the missile program, your wife, etc. *Russell Baker*

MADNESS. Permanent absent-mindedness.

MAGAZINE. Five pounds of advertisements mixed with fiction.
Cynic's Cyclopaedia

MAGNET. A thing you find in a bad apple. *Anon., Jr.*

MAID. A girl who hasn't been.
— A rare household pet.
　　OLD MAID. A woman who has been engaged once too seldom. *Cynic's Cyclopaedia*
　　— An unmarried woman who feels her oats and her corns at the same time. *Anon.*
　　— A girl of advanced years who has gone through life with no hits, no runs, and no errors—presumably. *Anon.*

MAILMAN. The contact man with the easy credit crowd.

MAJORITY. A few powerful leaders, a certain number of accommodating scoundrels and subservient weaklings, and a mass of men who trudge after them without in the least knowing their own minds. *Goethe*

MAKE-UP. A disguise used to make an actress look like her portraits.

— What makes you look happy when you're not.   *Anon., Jr.*

MAL DE MER. French for "you can't take it with you."
Garry Moore

MAN. The only animal that cooks.

— The only animal that spits.   *Donald A. Laird*

— The only animal who can strike a light.
Anon., Jr. (British Division)

— The only animal that blushes—or needs to.   *Mark Twain*

— The only animal that can be skinned more than once.
Irish Digest

— The only animal that can remain on friendly terms with the victims he intends to eat until he eats them.
Samuel Butler

— An animal that makes bargains; no other animal does this —no dog exchanges bones with another.   *Adam Smith*

— The only animal that is struck with the difference between what things are and what they ought to be.   *Hazlitt*

— The animal that intends to shoot himself out into interplanetary space, after having given up on the problem of an efficient way to get himself five miles or so to work and back each day.   *Bill Vaughan*

— An impossibility until he is born.   *R. W. Emerson*

— The inventor of stupidity.   *Remy de Gourmont*

— The earth has a skin and that skin has diseases; one of its diseases is called man.   *Nietzsche*

— The second strongest sex in the world.   *Philip Barry*

— Nature's sole mistake.   *Alexander Pope*

— A bundle of ancestors.   *Emerson*

— The organ of the accumulated smut and sneakery of 10,000 generations of weaseling souls.   *Philip Wylie*

— A creature made at the end of the week's work when God was tired.   *Mark Twain*

— A horse's best friend.

— A person who will pay two dollars for a one-dollar item he wants. A woman will pay one dollar for a two-dollar item she doesn't want. *William Binger*

— An animal split halfway up which walks on the split end.
Anon., Jr.

— A rational animal who always loses his temper when he is called upon to act in accordance with the dictates of reason. *Oscar Wilde*

— An imperfectly denatured animal intermittently subject to the unpredictable reactions of an unlocated spiritual area.
Rudyard Kipling

— A two-legged animal without feathers. *Plato*

— A somnolent animal made much of by women.

— A somewhat altered fish, a slightly remodeled ape.
George R. Stewart

— A political animal. *Aristotle*

— Of all the ways of defining man, the worst is the one which makes him out a rational animal. *Anatole France*

— A super-simian. *Elbert Hubbard*

— A somewhat elegant form of ape. *Anon.*

— An ape with possibilities. *Roy Chapman Andrews*

— A monkey who has learned to comb his hair.

— The difference between God and a monkey.

— A dog's ideal of what God should be. *Holbrook Jackson*

— The perfect beast. *Anon., Jr.*

— The king of beasts.

— The aristocrat amongst the animals. *Heine*

— An animal that throws peanuts to its ancestors.

— A box of wormseed. *Iver Brown*

— What a chimera is man! What a novelty, what a monster, what a chaos, what a contradiction, what a prodigy! . . . The glory and the shame of the universe. *Pascal*

MAN OF THE HOUR. The fellow whose wife told him to wait a minute.

SUCCESSFUL MAN. One who makes more money than his son at college can spend. *Anon. father*

WEALTHY OLD MAN. A labor-saving device. *Paul Gray*

MANKIND. Earthen jugs with spirits in them.

Nathaniel Hawthorne

— The most pernicious race of little odious vermin that nature ever suffered to crawl on the face of the earth.

Jonathan Swift

MANAGEMENT. A sense of direction.

MANAGERIE. The feminine of manager.

Anon., Jr. (British Division)

MANDATE. A male escort. *Anon. teenager*

MANDOLINES. High officials in China. *Anon., Jr.*

MANEUVER. What they put on grass. We have maneuver on our lawn. *Ibid.*

MANHATTAN. Seven million castaways on a raft.
— Seven million Rafts.

MANSION. Any house with a back stairway.

New England definition

MANUSCRIPT. Something submitted in haste and returned at leisure. *Oliver Herford*

MAPS. The shorthand of geography.

Gilbert Grosvenor, President
National Geographic Society

MARINATER. A herring aide.

MARINES. A small, fouled-up Army talking Navy lingo.

Brig. Gen. Frank Armstrong

MARKET. Three women and a goose. *Italian proverb*

MARRIAGE. The greatest adventure of all. *McCall's*
— A friendship recognized by the police.

Robert Louis Stevenson

— A public confession of a strictly private intention.

James C. Dayenhart

— An institution which is popular because it combines the maximum of temptation with the maximum of opportunity.
George Bernard Shaw

— A book of which the first chapter is written in poetry and the remaining chapters in prose. *Beverley Nichols*

— The thing that makes loving legal. *Simone Signoret*

— A souvenir of love. *Helen Rowland*

— The only known example of the happy meeting of the immovable object and the irresistible force. *Ogden Nash*

— Would be heavenly if the first night lasted forever.
Anon. widow

— A perfect moment frozen for a dull eternity. *Bill Manville*

— An armed alliance against the outside world.
G. K. Chesterton

— The alliance of two people one of whom never remembers birthdays and the other never forgets them. *Ogden Nash*

— All your money down and the rest of your life to pay.

— A woman's hair net tangled in a man's spectacles on top of the bedroom dresser. *Don Herold*

— A pair of shears, so joined that they cannot be separated; often moving in opposite directions, yet always punishing anyone who comes between them. *Sydney Smith*

— An institution that simplifies life and complicates living.
Jean Rostand

— Love under quarantine.

— A long quarrel. *French proverb*

— A deal in which a man gives away half his groceries in order to get the other half cooked. *John Gwynne*

— A constant test to determine if the husband is faster on the deposit than the wife is on the draw. *Robert Q. Lewis*

— The most expensive hobby. *Justice H. G. Wenzel*

— A community consisting of a master, a mistress, and two slaves—making in all two. *Ambrose Bierce*

— A business in which a man takes his boss along on his vacation.

— A two-handed game of solitaire. *Anon.*

— One long conversation, chequered by disputes.
Robert Louis Stevenson

— A lot like playing the horses. It all depends on how lucky you are at the $2 window. *Robert Q. Lewis*

— A lottery in which men stake their liberty and women their happiness. *M. Rieux*

— A quiz show you lose if you give the right answer.
Anon. husband

— The union you join when you labor under a delusion.

— Not a word but a sentence. *Anon.*

— A word which should be pronounced "mirage."
Herbert Spencer

— A snore and a delusion. *Anon.*

— A period during which a man finds out what sort of fellow his wife would have preferred. *The Vagabonds*

— Working for nothing. *Irish maid*

— A fire-extinguisher.

— The most expensive way to get your laundry done free.
Charley Jones

— A scheme for looting the male. *Nord Riley*

— The chief cause of divorce. *Anon., Jr.*

— A romance in which the hero dies in the first chapter.
Anon.

— The end of man. *Balzac.*

MARRIAGE LAWS. Along with police, armies and navies, the mark of human incompetence. *Mrs. Bertrand Russell*

MARRIED. Marred. *Shakespeare*

MARRY. To domesticate the Recording Angel.
Robert Louis Stevenson

MARRYING. Putting one's hand into a bag of snakes on the chance of drawing out an eel. *Leonardo da Vinci*

SECOND MARRIAGE. The triumph of hope over experience.
Dr. Samuel Johnson

MARTYR. A self-made hero.

— A pile of wood set on fire with a man on top. *Anon., Jr.*

MARTYRDOM. The only way in which a man can become famous without ability. *George Bernard Shaw*

MARX BROTHERS. All gall, divided into three parts.
                                        *Robertson White**
GROUCHO MARX. A racketeer who got into show business.
                                        Groucho Marx

MASKED BALL. A charitable entertainment for ladies of plain
   features.   *Cynic's Cyclopaedia*

MASOCHIST. Someone who builds dungeons in the air.
                                        Celeste Holm

MASON-DIXON LINE. The boundary between you-all and
   youse.   Anon.

MASSES. Population in the raw.

MASTICATION. What the Italians do with their hands when
   they talk English.   Anon., Jr.

MATCH-MAKING. Putting one and one together to make another one.

MATERNITY HOSPITAL. A delivery stable.
— An heirport.   *Peter Donald*
— A place of confinement.

MATHEMATICIAN. A man who can figure his own income tax.
                                        Cynic's Cyclopaedia
MATHEMATICS. The music of reason.   *J. J. Sylvester*
— The subject in which we never know what we are talking
   about, nor whether what we are saying is true.
                                        Bertrand Russell
— A wonderful science, but it hasn't yet come up with a
   way to divide one tricycle between three small boys.
                                        Earl Wilson
MATRIMONY. A process that makes strange bedfellows.
                                        Groucho Marx
— An insane desire on a man's part to pay a woman's board.
                                        Anon.

— The only state left in which practically everything is legal.
Nancy Randolph

— A bargain, and somebody has to get the worst of the bargain.
Helen Rowland

— A process by which the grocer gets an account the haberdasher once had.
Franklin D. Roosevelt

— A figurative ship of which the husband is the figurative captain.

— A repast in the Chinese style, starting with the sweetmeat and ending in the soup.

— The root of all evil.
Ethel Watts Mumford

— A place where souls suffer for a time on account of their sins.
Anon., Jr.

— A state of terrible torment which those who enter are compelled to undergo for a time to prepare them for a better world.
Anon., Jr.

MAUGHAM, W. SOMERSET. The kind of man who has seen everything and doesn't think much of any of it.   *Karsh*

MAUSOLEUM. A filing cabinet for closed correspondence.

MAUVE. Pink trying to be purple.   *James McN. Whistler*

MAXIM SILENCER. Voltaire.

MAXWELL, ELSA. Society's leading performing seal.   *Anon.*

MAY. The month the old-clothes man swindles your wife out of your overcoat.   *Abe Martin*

MAYOR. A he horse.   *Anon., Jr.*

McCARTHY, CHARLIE. A wood-wind instrument.   *Jan Peerce*

MEALTIME. When the children sit down to continue eating.

MEAT. Grass once removed.

MECHANIC. A man who thinks with a monkey wrench.

MEDAL. Scrap iron. *Thomas W. Jackson*
— A pat on the chest.
— Coinage for carnage.
— An award given for saving or destroying life.

MEDICINE. A drug on the market.

MEDIUM. A party with one ear to the grave but both hands
on your wallet. *Foolish Dictionary*
— A big wheel with spooks.

MEISTERSINGER. A Middle Age crooner.

MELANCHOLY. The pleasure of being sad. *Victor Hugo*

MELBA. The place where Napoleon was imprisoned.
Anon., Jr. (British Division)

MELODRAMA. Drama aged in the wood.

MEMOIRS. What a person went through that everybody ought
to know.

MEMORY. A beaten path in the brain.
— A sieve in which we try to keep knowledge.
— What a man forgets with when he owes you money.
Anon. Irishman
— A hidden chord that is touched when we listen to our
friends' original stories. *Cynic's Cyclopaedia*

MEN. Animals used by words. *James Branch Cabell*
— The cause of women's dislike for one another.
La Bruyère
— What women marry. *Anon., Jr. (British Division)*
"MEN WANTED". The best sign of prosperity. *Kin Hubbard*

MENCKEN, H. L. Nietzsche with a saxophone. *Frank Fenton*

MENU. A list of dishes the restaurant has just run out of.

MEPHISTOPHELES. A Greek comic poet. *Anon., Jr.*

MERCURY. The god of weather, because it is in thermometers.

Anon., Jr.

MERMAID. A pin-up tadpole.

— An oomph girl upstairs and a fish downstairs.   *Anon.*

— A wet dream.

MERRY-GO-ROUND. A vehicle for getting nowhere quickly.

MESS CALL. The battle cry of feed 'em.

METAPHOR. A suppressed smile.   *Anon., Jr.*

— A thing you shout through.   *Ibid., Jr.*

— A strong way of saying polite things, such as would be called swearing by uneducated people

Anon., Jr. (British Division)

METAPHYSICS. A debate on whether the debaters exist and, if so, why?

— An attempt to establish an alibi for the universe.

METEOROLOGIST. A man who can look into a girl's eyes and tell whether.   *Anon.*

THE METHOD. Acting on an impulse.

METHUSELAH. The snake in the Garden of Eden.   *Anon., Jr.*

METRONOME. A midget who works for MGM.

According to a girl Bob Scott told Edith Gwynn he knows.

METROPOLIS. Any city with Childs on the corner—and no children on the street.   *Dorothy Gulman**

MICKEY FINN. A liquid blackjack.   *Jack Benny*

— The Drink Evil.

MICROBE. A robe that the mics wear.

Anon., Jr., (British Division)

MIDDLE OF THE ROAD. Precisely the place where one gets hit by cars coming from both directions.   *Charles Frankel*

MIDDLE AGE. That time of life when the average man is going to begin saving next month. *Wally Maher*

— When you're not inclined to exercise anything but caution. *Arthur Murray*

— When work is no longer play and play is getting to be work. *Art Moger*

— The time when a man is always thinking that in a week or two he will feel just as good as ever. *Don Marquis*

— The time when you'll do anything to feel better, except give up what's hurting you. *Robert Quillen*

— That period when a man begins to feel friendly toward insurance agents. *The Wyatt Way*

— The time a guy starts turning out the lights for economical rather than romantic reasons. *John Marino*

— When you're willing to get up and give your seat to a lady—and can't. *Sammy Kaye*

— When you can do just as much as ever, but would rather not.

— Having a choice of two temptations and choosing the one that will get you home earlier. *Dan Bennett*

— When you are sitting at home on Saturday night and the telephone rings and you hope it isn't for you. *Ring Lardner*

— When your wife tells you to pull in your stomach and you already have! *Jack Barry*

— When you have met so many people that every new person you meet reminds you of someone else and usually is. *Ogden Nash*

— When you decide you look a lot handsomer in glasses.

— Later than you think and sooner than you expect. *Earl Wilson*

— When a woman's hair starts turning from gray to black.

MIDDLE-AGED. Ten years older than you are. *Anon.*

MIDDLE AGES. The roaring forties. *R. W. Dawson*

MIDDLEMAN. One who works both ends against the middle. *Elbert Hubbard*

— One who gets it in the end.

MILITARY. That which is not civil.   *Talleyrand*
   MILITARY EXPERT. A man who tells you today what is going
      to happen tomorrow, and who tells you tomorrow why
      it didn't happen today.   *John Charles Thomas*
   MILITARY FAME. To be killed in the field of battle and have
    our names spelled wrong in the newspapers.
              Gen. William Tecumseh Sherman

MILLENNIUM. Something like a centennial, only it has more
   legs.   *Anon., Jr.*

MILLION DOLLARS. A sum that may be honestly acquired by
   putting aside $500 out of one's salary every week for
   forty years.

MILLIONAIRE SPORTSMAN. A bum whose creditors haven't
   caught him.   *Jimmy Cannon*

MIND. A cloud no bigger than a man's brain.
— No matter.
   (Compare MATTER: Never mind.)

MINE. A hole in the ground owned by a liar.
                 Foolish Dictionary

MINISTER. The man who collects the "I do's" for the union.

MINK. When a woman turns around to look at another woman
   —that's mink.   *Macy's*
   MINK COAT. A woman's reward for indifference.
                 Oscar Levant

MINNEAPOLIS. A suburb—according to St. Paul.

MINNESOTA. A state that has 10,000 lakes and 1,000 fish.
                 Cedric Adams
— A state with two seasons, winter and autumn.

MINUET. You and I have dined.   *Charlestonese*

MINUTEMAN. One who can dash into the kitchen and prepare
   a sandwich before the TV commercial's over.
                 George Hart

MIRACLE. An event described by those to whom it was told by men who did not see it. *Elbert Hubbard*
MIRACLE DRUG. Any drug you can get the kids to take without screaming. *Bob Merrill*

MIRAGE. A free movie.

MIRROR. The portrait of your enemy.

MIRTH. Fun shaking the laughter out of you. *David Garrick*

MISADVENTURE. An adventure with a miss.

MISE. To act the part of a miser. *Anon.*

MISER. One who or that which mises. *A. T. Pope*
— One who is miserable. *Tyron Edwards*
— A man suffering from an ingrown income.
— One who eats mice. *Anon., Jr.*

MISERY. A miser's bedfellow.

MISFORTUNE. The kind of fortune that never misses.
Cynic's Cyclopaedia

MISSISSIPPI. A state with 226,356 Methodists, 441,293 Baptists, and the lowest literacy rate in America.
H. L. Mencken

MISTAKES. The world's principal product.

MISTLETOE. The astronaut's athlete's foot. *Anon.*

MISTRESS. Something that goes between mister and mattress.
Joe E. Lewis°

MOAN. To howl under one's breath.

MOB. The scum that rises when the water boils. *Anon.*

MODERN. A word often used to justify what has no other merit. *Anon.*
MODERN ART. Oodles of doodles. *Lawrence Braun*

MODESTY. The gentle art of enhancing your charm by pretending not to be aware of it. *Oliver Herford*

— The feeling that others will surely discover in a little while just how wonderful you are.

MODISTE. A dressmaker with a label.

MOHAMMED. A mountain climber.

MOISTY. The opposite of thirsty.

MOLDING. A belt around a room.

MOLECULE. A girlish boy. *Anon., Jr.*

MOLOTOV. The best filing clerk in Russia. *Lenin*

MOMENTUM. What you give a person when they are leaving. *Anon., Jr.*

MONARCH. A king with a good publicity man.

MONASTERIES. Places where monsters were kept. *Anon., Jr.*

MONDAY MORNING. That's when we look back wistfully on the good old days—Saturday and Sunday. *Catholic Digest*

MONEY. Time. *George Gissing*
— Tokens of perspiration.
— One of the strangest things about life is that the poor, who need money the most, are the very ones that never have it. *Finley Peter Dunne*
— An article which may be used as a universal passport to everywhere except heaven, and as a universal provider of everything except happiness. *Wall Street Journal*
— A good thing to have. It frees you from doing things you dislike. Since I dislike doing nearly everything, money is handy. *Groucho Marx*

MONEYLENDER. One who would tear the skin off a flea. *Russian proverb*

MONGOOSE. A Scotch gander.

MONKEY. A malicious mirror.

MONOCLE. A pane of glass in an empty window.   *Anon.*

MONOGAMY. A marriage system in which subscribers are requested to return one wife before taking another.

MONOLOGUE. A conversation between several hundred students and a professor.   *Washington Columns*
— A conversation between two people, such as a husband and wife.   *Anon., Jr.*
— A conversation between a realtor and a prospect.   *Judge*
— A conversation with a girl.   *College Humor*
   MONOLOGIST. A man with a lonely occupation: you stand on the stage talking to yourself, being overheard by an audience.   *Fred Allen*

MONOPOLY. The practice of first come, take all.
   MONOPOLIST. A man who keeps an elbow on each arm of his theatre chair.   *Anon.*

MONOTONY. Having only one wife at a time.   *Anon., Jr.*

MONROE DOCTRINE. A standing offer to grown men of a ride in a perambulator.   *Philip Guedalla*

MONSIEUR. The difference between Madame and Mademoiselle.   *Phyllis Farrar*

MONSOON. A typhoon that's going steady with a tornado.
          Bob Hope
— A French gentleman.   *Anon., Jr.*

MONTE CARLO. An ocean dive.

MONTH. Around the world on a moonbeam.

MONUMENT. A boast in stone.

MOO. The conversation of contented cows.

MOON. The earth's yo-yo.
— A planet just like the earth, only deader.   *Anon., Jr.*

MOORE, GEORGE. An author who wrote brilliant English until he discovered grammar. *Oscar Wilde*
— An author with no enemies, although none of his friends like him. *William Butler Yeats*

MOOSE. A Scotch mouse.

MORAL INDIGNATION. Suppressed envy.
— Jealousy with a halo. *H. G. Wells*

MORALITY. The attitude we adopt towards people whom we personally dislike. *Oscar Wilde*
— Drawing the line somewhere. *G. K. Chesterton*
— Low blood pressure. *J. Taylor & C. O. Spencer*
MORALITY PLAY. A play in which the characters are goblins, ghosts, virgins, and other supernatural creatures.
Anon., Jr.

MORALS. Just a matter of pulling down the window shades.
Professor Swayzee

MORATORIUM. A big ocean liner. *Anon., Jr.*

MORMON. A man that has the bad taste and the religion to do what a good many other men are restrained from doing by conscientious scruples and the police. *Mr. Dooley*

MORNING. The time of day when the rising generation retires and the retiring generation rises. *Alexander Animator*

MOROCCO. A cold country with a hot sun.
Marshal Louis Lyautey

MORON. One who is content with a serene mind.
College Humor

MORTGAGE. An I O U with blackjack attached.

MORTUARY. A place where the dead are prepared for the living.

MOSAIC. A jigsaw puzzle in stone.

Mosquito. The child of black and white parents. *Anon., Jr.*
mosquitoes. The inhabitants of Moscow. *Ibid.*

Moth. A poor butterfly.
— A perverse creature that spends the summer in a fur coat and the winter in a bathing suit. *Anon.*

Mother-in-Law. A mother who makes the laws in a family.
Anon., Jr.

Motherhood. An incident, an occupation, or a career according to the mettle of the woman.

Motion Picture. A business of making mud pies and playing Indian. *Grover Jones*
— Art simplified, purified, and hog-tied.
— The new literature. *Cecil B. DeMille°*

Mountain. An affront to man's conquest of nature.
Edward Whymper, first conqueror of the Matterhorn
mountain climber. An athlete who will climb to any heights to get a nosebleed. *Anon.*
mountain pass. A pass given by railroads to their employees so that they can spend their vacation in the mountains. *Anon., Jr.*
mountain range. A cooking stove used at high altitudes.
Anon., Jr. (British Division)

Mouth. A hole under a drunkard's nose that all his money runs into. *English proverb*

Movie Actress. Just a plain girl who's beautiful. *Ed Gardner*

Movie Short. A film that only runs two hours. *Earl Wilson*

Movie Star. Somebody who's just like the boy next door— if you live in Beverly Hills. *Tom Jenk*
— A guy with a swimming pool and a worried look.
Bob Hope

MOVIES. A place where people talk behind your back.
Ford Islander

MR. Short for Monster. *Don Herold*

MUDDLE. A beautiful chick who poses in pitchers.
New Yorkese

MUEZZIN. A Mohammedan church bell.

MUGWUMP. A bird that sits on the fence with its mug on one side and its wump on the other. *Abraham Lincoln*

MUMMIES. The inhabitants of ancient Egypt. *Anon., Jr.*

MUNITIONS MANUFACTURERS. Patriots who want to sell us rifles for protection against foreign powers to whom they have already sold cannons. *Leo C. Rosten*

MURDER. A widely prevalent act which should either be discouraged or legalized. *Anon.*
— Retroactive birth control.
— Glorified assault. *Arthur Train*
   MURDERER. One who takes life too easily.
   — A man who is supposed to be innocent until he is proved insane. *Reader's Digest*

MUSEUM. A place full of stuffed people.
Linda Carol Levinson*
— A dead circus. *Anon., Jr.*

MUSHROOMS. Vegetables which grow in damp places and so they always look like umbrellas. *Anon., Jr.*

MUSIC. Liquid architecture.
— Noise with discipline.
— Love in search of a word. *Sidney Lanier*
— The shorthand of emotion. *Tolstoy*
— The speech of angels. *Thomas Carlyle*
— A habit, like smoking or spitting. *Percy Grainger*
— Another lady that talks charmingly and says nothing.
Austin O'Malley

CLASSICAL MUSIC. The kind that we keep hoping will turn into a tune. *Abe Martin*

COOL MUSICIAN. One who flats his fifth.

DIXIELAND MUSICIAN. One who drinks his. *Anon.*

MUSIC LOVER. A man, who upon hearing a soprano in the bathroom, puts his ear to the keyhole. *Kalends*

MUSSET, ALFRED DE. A young man with a brilliant future behind him. *Heinrich Heine*

MUSSOLINI, BENITO. A man possible only in a country that has no appreciation of real acting. *Leo Lania*
— That unfortunate gorilla. *John Gunther*

MUTUEL CLERK. A horse player who is paid for spending the afternoon at the races. *Jimmy Cannon*

MYTH. A story that everyone accepts but no one believes.
— A long-term fib.
— A female moth. *Anon., Jr.*

N

NAG. A woman who has a mule for a husband.

Reader's Digest

NAKED. Without benefit of missionary.
NAKEDNESS. The homely with their clothes off.

NAPKIN. A lapkerchief.
— A little nap.
— A cloth that leaves its nap on your lap.

NASTY. Not a nice word (see NICE). *George Bernard Shaw*

NATION, CARRIE. A good woman in the worst sense of the word.

NATIONAL DEBT. America's most outstanding public figure.

Joseph B. Young

NATIONALISM. An infantile disease. It is the measles of mankind. *Albert Einstein*

NATURAL. Untamed.

NAUSEA. An island in the Aegean Sea. *Anon., Jr.*

NAZISM. The St. Vitus dance of the Twentieth Century.

Hermann Rauschning

NEATNESS. The one thing good about being bald. *Anon.*

NECESSITY. Yesterday's luxury.
— The mother of convention. *Anon., Jr. (British Division)*

NECK. To conduct an experiment in comparative physiology.

NEGLIGEE. What she hopes she'll have on when the house burns down. *Macy's*

NEIGHBOR. A person who can get to your house in less than a minute and take two hours to go back home.

O. A. Battista

— A person who borrows. *Anon., Jr.*

NEPOTISM. A $10 word meaning to stow your relatives in a soft berth. *Ilka Chase*

NERO. A Roman candle burner.

NETS. Holes surrounded by pieces of string.

Anon., Jr. (British Division)

NETWORK. Anything reticulated and decussated at equal distances with interstices at the intersections.

Dr. Samuel Johnson

NEUTRALITY. Not taking sides in public.

NEVERGREEN. The opposite of evergreen. *Anon., Jr.*

NEW YEAR'S DAY. Every man's birthday. *Charles Lamb*

NEW YORK CITY. The city of Brotherly Shove.

Dallas Townsend

— An island in the Atlantic. *Waldo Frank*

— A nightmare in stone. *Edgar Saltus, 1906*

— Hamburgerville-on-the-run. *Elizabeth Hawley**

— A city of 7,000,000, so decadent that when I leave it I never dare look back lest I turn into salt and the conductor throw me over his left shoulder for good luck.

Frank Sullivan

— A place where everyone will stop watching a championship fight to look at an usher giving a drunk the bum's rush.

Damon Runyon

— The Hollywood version of a metropolis.

— A good place to hide. *Anon., Jr.*

NEW YORKERS. People who get acquainted with their neighbors by meeting them in Miami. *Marjorie Steele*

NEW ZEALAND. A democratic country where they passed a law preventing women from sweating in the factories.

Anon., Jr.

NEWLYWED. A man who puts up the storm windows the first time his wife suggests it.

NEWS. The disasters of the day. *Anon.*
— The same thing happening every day to different people.
The Era
— Nobody's business in print.
— Anything that makes a woman say: "For heaven's sake!"
Ed Howe

NEWS BROADCAST. Airing the world's linen.

NEWSPAPER. A portable screen behind which a man hides from the woman who is standing up in a street car.
Los Angeles *Times*
— A conspiracy to suppress the facts of life.
— A circulating library with high blood pressure.
Arthur "Bugs" Baer
— A device for amusing one half of the world with the other half's troubles.

NEWSPAPERS. The mouth-organs of the people. *Anon., Jr.*

NEWSREEL. A medium which presents the public man pitilessly, warts and all. *Valentine Williams*

NEXT WEEK. The week after, if you're lucky.
— The time when a good picture is coming to the movie theatre.

NIAGARA FALLS. Water on the rocks.
— The bride's second great disappointment. *Anon. bride*

NICE. A nasty word. *George Bernard Shaw*

NIGHT CLUB. An unrestaurant. *Anon.*
— An ash tray with music. *Coronet*
— A saloon with an orchestra. *Matt Weinstock*
— A place where people with nothing to remember go to forget. *Grove Patterson*
— A place where the tables are reserved and the guests aren't. *Fred Casper*

— The only place in the world where you pay $11 for a ringside seat and do all the fighting yourself.
Arthur "Bugs" Baer

NIGHT CLUB BOUNCER. A man who throws noisy parties.
Lee Carpenter

NIGHT WATCHMAN. A man employed to sleep in the open air.
Cecil Hunt

NIGHTINGALE, FLORENCE. A French opera singer, who sang to the soldiers during the French and Indian war. *Anon., Jr.*

NIXON, RICHARD. The fearless champion of the overdog.

No. The feminine of yes. *Cynic's Cyclopaedia*

NOAH. I saw him as a kind of supervisor—a building contractor. *Igor Stravinsky*

NOBBISH. A stylish nebbish. *Anon.*

NOBEL, ALFRED B. A man who endowed the world with dynamite and prizes to discourage its use.

NOBILITY. One who has no ability. *Anon., Jr.*

NOISE. Audible grime.

NOM DE GUERRE. A fighting name.

NOM DE PLUME. A writing name.

NONAGENARIAN. A man who makes the same mistakes he did at eighty.

NONCOMBATANT. A dead Quaker. *Ambrose Bierce*

NONENTITY. A zero with the rim taken off.
Prof. M. B. Garrett

NOOK. A niche for learning.

NOON. The hour when bushes tuck shade beneath them like skirts.   *D. C. Peattie*

NOOSE. The tie that binds.

NORMAL. Having the usual eccentricities.

NORTH AFRICA. Texas with Arabs.   *Anon.*

NORTH CAROLINA. A valley of humility between two mountains of conceit.   *Anon.*

NORWAY. Sweden without matches.   *Charlie McCarthy*

NOSE. The bone and gristle penthouse.   *Stewart Robertson*

NOSTALGIA. That which makes things seem a hundred times more wonderful now than they did when they were taking place.   *Walter Slezak*

NOTARY. One who takes in swearing for a living.*

NOTE. A memo at random.   *Anon.*

NOUN. (Abstract) Something you can't see when you are looking at it.   *Anon., Jr. (British Division)*

NOVEL. ("Beat") Take a lot of brothel scenes, a bit of marihuana, some bad poetry and some bleating; add a few dishes of Oriental philosophy and some cool jazz; let it set until it grows a small beard, and there you are!
                                                          Robert Fontaine
— (Historical) Like a bustle, a fictitious tale covering up a stern reality.   *Augusta Tucker*
   NOVELIST. In the old days, a spare-time genius. Nowadays, a man who can write 2,000 words a day on the same subject.

---

* Subscribed and sworn before me this 1st day of April, 1962, (Sig.) Samuel Pollack, Notary Public, State of New York, No. 31–8402250, Qualified in New York County, Commission Expires March 30, 1964.

— A sort of itinerant glazier, transporting a mirror along the highway of the world to reflect impartially its sunsets and mud puddles.

Nineteenth-century conception,
according to Donald Malcolm

NOVEMBER. The fog of the year. *Mark Van Doren*

Now. Too late. *Bill Manville*

NUDISM. Life in the raw.
    NUDIST. One who has acquired nothing since birth except nerve. *Ken Taylor**
— One who suffers from clothestrophobia.

Robert Q. Lewis

    NUDIST CAMPS. Started by a group of sunbathers who, in their search for a perfect tan, were determined to leave no stern untoned. *Charles Dwelley*
    NUDIST COLONY. A place where you peel first and get sunburn after.

NUMB. A sensation you feel when you don't.

NUMBER. A pen-name. *Santa Fe magazine*

NUMERALS. Symbols used in a form of lying called statistics.

NUMEROLOGY. The numbers racket. *Fibber McGee*

NUMISMATICS. Collecting money for fun.

NURSE. A woman whose business is to make sickness a pleasure.
    NURSE'S AIDE. A girl who can make the patient without disturbing the bed. *Anon.**

NUT. A fruit built like an oyster. *Penrose Coed*

O

O.K. Yes in two words.

OAF. An old-fashioned jerk.

OATS. A grain which in England is generally given to horses, but in Scotland supports the people. *Dr. Samuel Johnson*

OBESE. Over 300 pounds.

OBLIVION. The hell of a good idea.

OBOE. An ill woodwind that nobody blows good. *Drexerd*
— An American tramp. *Anon., Jr. (British Division)*

OBSTACLE. A difficulty you see when you take your eyes off the goal. *Anon.*

OBSTINACY. Error in armor.

OCCIDENTATION. A word that hasn't been invented yet. When I decide what to do with it, I'll let you know.
— On second thought, it's orientation toward the West.

OCEAN. A large body of water entirely surrounded by trouble. *Enka Voice*

OCEANICA. That continent which contains no land. *Anon., Jr.*

OCCUPATION. The principal thing one engages in to avoid thinking.

OCTOGENARIAN. A man who makes the same mistakes he did at seventy.
— An animal which has eight young at a birth. *Anon., Jr.*

OCTOPUS. A fish built like a corporation.
— A person who hopes for the best.   *Anon., Jr.*

OCTOROON. An eight-legged, pink spider.   *Anon., Jr.*

OCULIST. A fish with long pegs. *Anon., Jr. (British Division)*

ODD. Uneven.

ODOR. A bad smell.
   ODOUR. A nice smell.

OFFICIAL SCORER. A baseball writer who decides hits and errors while looking at his typewriter in the press box.
            Jimmy Cannon

OGRE. A frightful bore.

OIL. A product that can smooth the sea and upheave the land.

OLD. Familiar.
   OLD AGE. An incurable disease.   *Seneca*
   — When all girls look alike to you.   *Mac Benoff*
   — The time of life when you awaken in the morning and say "Am I still here?"
   — Fifteen years older than I am.   *Bernard Baruch*
   — When you stop wondering how to dodge temptation and start wondering if you're missing any.   *Earl Wilson*
   — When it's not so hard to avoid temptation as it is to find it.   *Cosmo Sardo*
   — That period when you feel your oats and your corns at the same time.   *H. G. Hutcheson*
   OLD-TIMER. One who can recall when a bureau was a piece of furniture.   *Carey MacWilliams*
   — A fellow who remembers when, if a woman had to be carried out of a place, she had either fainted or died.
            Abe Martin
   — The one who can recall when a man wasn't called a reactionary when he said a good word for free enterprise.
           Calgary Albertan
   — One who can remember when a juvenile delinquent was a kid who owed eight cents on an overdue library book.

OLD-TIMER'S GAME. A game in which veteran athletes get paid nothing to build up a profit for a multimillion dollar corporation. *Jimmy Cannon*

OLD WEST. A place where men were men and smelled like horses. *Judy Canova*

OLEOMARGARINE. Something you have to take for butter or worse. *Betty Cass*

OLYMPIC GAMES. Contests consisting of running races, jumping, hurdling the biscuits, and throwing the java. The reward to the victor is a coral reef. *Anon., Jr.*

OMEN. Invisible handwriting on the wall.

OMNIBUS. A four-wheeled vehicle for two-legged cattle.

OPERA. An exotic and irrational entertainment.
Dr. Samuel Johnson
— Music set to melodrama.
— A magic scene contrived to please the eyes and the ears at the expense of the understanding. *Lord Chesterfield*
— When a guy gets stabbed in the back and instead of bleeding he sings. *Ed Gardner*
— A form of entertainment where there's always too much singing. *Claude Debussy*
    MET OPERA OPENING. An occasion where there are 25,000 people—all pushing me. *I. L. Myers*
    OPERA SINGERS. Peasants with God-given voices.
Mme. Frances Alda

OPERATION. An attempt to repair the machine without stopping the motor.
    MINOR OPERATION. One that was performed on the other fellow. *Russel Pettis Askue*

OPINION. The thought of the month.

OPPORTUNITY. Something that goes without saying.
    OPPORTUNIST. One who opens the door before Opportunity can knock.
    — One who goes ahead and does what you always intended to do. *K. L. Krichbaum*

OPTIMISM. The belief that all peas are sweetpeas.

OPTIMIST. An anti-skeptic.

— A person who believes that a housefly is looking for a way to get out. *George Jean Nathan*

— A man who gets treed by a lion but enjoys the scenery. *Walter Winchell*

— A person who says the bottle is half full when it is half empty. *Anon. pessimist*

— A guy who doesn't care what happens, as long as it doesn't happen to him. *Curt Bois*

— A man who marries his secretary thinking he'll continue to dictate to her. *Typo Graphic*

— A guy who thinks his wife has quit smoking cigarettes when he finds cigar butts around the house. *Anon.*

— A guy who can always see the bright side of other people's troubles. *Mac Benoff*

— A fellow who digs dandelions out of his lawn. *Kin Hubbard*

— The fellow who talks about what a fool he used to be. *Buddy Satz*

— A man who hasn't got around to reading the morning papers. *Earl Wilson*

— A woman who thinks the man she's about to marry is better than the one she just divorced. *Jacques Belasco*

— Anybody who expects change. *John J. Plomp*

— One who proclaims that we live in the best of all possible worlds. A pessimist fears that this is true. *James Branch Cabell*

— Girl who mistakes a bulge for a curve. *Ring Lardner*

— Someone who tells you to cheer up when things are going his way. *Edward R. Murrow*

— A guy who has never had much experience. *Don Marquis*

— A bridegroom who thinks he has no bad habits. *Klavan and Finch*

— A man who looks after your eyes; a pessimist looks after your feet. *Anon., Jr. (British Division)*

OPTIMIST CLUB. An organization of businessmen who are generally too old to belong to the Boy Scouts.

Elliott Arnold

ORACLE. A volcano giving amphibious answers. *Anon., Jr.*

ORATORY. Platitudes plus personality. *Amos R. Wells*
— The only career that gives a man a woman's privileges.
— A solitary vice performed in public.
— An appeal to the emotions by beating the eardrums.
— The art of making deep sounds from the chest seem like important messages from the brain.

ORGAN. A petrified bagpipe.
ORGAN GRINDER. One who walks around with a chimp on his shoulder. *Don Quinn**

ORIENT. The Far East. In the U.S.A. it's New England.

ORIGINAL. Copied unconsciously.
ORIGINALITY. Judicious imitation. *Voltaire*
— Undetected plagiarism. *Dean Inge*

ORPHANS. Prisoners of charity. *Joseph Harrington*

ORPHEUS. The husband of Aurora; therefore her god.
Anon., Jr.

ORTHODOX. A religion in China which doesn't allow people to eat Buddah with their meat. *Anon., Jr.*

OSLO. The biggest village in Norway. *Anon.*

OSTRACIZED. An ostrich who sticks his head in the sand when he thinks someone is coming. *Anon., Jr.*

OTTER. Exterior, as in "Otter spays." *New Yorkese*

OUCH! The class yell of the School of Experience.
Walter Winchell

OUTBOARD MOTORBOAT. A rowboat with athlete's phut.
Anon. collegiate

OUTER SPACE. Our large suburb.   *Charles Poore*

OVEREATING. An activity which will make you thick to your stomach.   *Charley Jones*

OVERT ACT. Knocking the chip off a nation's shoulder.

OWNER. The one with the right to say who can use a thing.

OX. A cow that can't have babies.   *Anon., Jr.*

OXYGEN. The plural of ox.   *Anon., Jr.*

OXONIAN. A man who drives a pair of oxes.   *Anon., Jr.*

OZARKS. The worst outdoor slums in the United States.   *Anon.*

P

PACIFIST. A guy who fights with everybody but the enemy.
Anon.

— A flag-waiver.

PACKING. Maneuvering an auto to the curb.
Charlestonese

PAINE, THOMAS. A rare individual obsessed by common sense.
Anon., Jr.

PAINTER. Someone who founds his art collection by painting it himself.
PAINTING. Doodling as a profession.
— Deaf poetry.   *Simoneds*
— Another way of keeping a diary.   *Pablo Picasso*

PAJAMAS. Garments that newlyweds place beside the bed in case of fire.   *Kay Norton**

PAL. An acquaintance who is about to do you a favor.

PALM BEACH. A place where people go in the winter to blackball each other from membership in the beach clubs.
Leslie Hore-Belisha

PALM SPRINGS. The sandbox of society.   *Bee Nicoll*

PALSY. A kind of new writer's dance.
Anon., Jr. (British Division)

PAMPHLET. A book in short pants.

PANACEA. A temple dedicated to all the gods.   *Anon., Jr.*

PAN-AMERICANISM. The practice of protecting our customers from our competitors.

PANDEMONIUM. A din of iniquity.

PANIC. A rumor on fire.

PANORAMIC VIEW. Real estatese for "A view of the house across the street."   *William V. Shannon*

PANTIES. Pants plus tease.
— Curtains for the sitting room.   *Lehigh Burr*

PAPAL BULL. A cow that was kept at the Vatican to supply milk for the Pope's children.   *Anon., Jr.*
— A mad bull kept by the Pope in the Inquisition to trample on Protestants.   *Anon., Jr.*

PARABLE. A heavenly story with no earthly meaning.
          Anon., Jr. (British Division)

PARACHUTE. A device that makes it possible to walk back from an airplane ride.

PARADISE. An amusement park for those who have died.

PARAFFIN. The next order of angels above the Seraphim.
          Anon., Jr.

PARASITE. A male inhabitant of Paris.   *Anon., Jr.*
— The murder of an infant.   *Anon., Jr.*
— The lesser of two weevils.
— Great fleas have little fleas upon their backs to bite 'em,
  And little fleas have lesser fleas, and so on ad infinitum.

  And the great fleas themselves in turn have greater fleas to grow on,
  While these again have greater still and greater still and so on.   *De Morgan*

PARATROOPER. A soldier who climbs down trees he never climbs up.   *Anon.*

PARENT. One who thinks he is old enough to know better.
— Children aren't happy with nothing to ignore,
  And that's what parents were created for.   *Ogden Nash*

PARENTS. People who use the rhythm system of birth control. *Mary Flink*
— The hardships of a minor's life. *Coronet*

PARENTHESES. A barrel for a thought that lost its suspenders.

PARIS. The place where a man who has money to burn meets
his match.
— A city of gaieties and pleasures where four fifths of the
inhabitants die of grief. *Nicholas Chamfort*

PARKING LOT. A place where you leave your car to have dents
put in the fenders. *Coronet*

PARKING SPACE. An unoccupied area that's always on the
other side of the street. *Mac Benoff*

PARLIAMENT. A big meeting of more or less idle people.
Walter Bagehot

PARROT. A mocking bird. *Cynic's Cyclopaedia*
— A bird with the ability to imitate man, but not the brains
to refrain from doing so.
— The only creature gifted with the power of speech that is
content to repeat just what it hears without trying to make
a good story out of it. *Anon. collegiate*

PARSIFAL. The kind of opera that starts at six o'clock and
after it has been going three hours, you look at your watch
and it says 6:20. *David Randolph*

PARSIMONY. Money left by your father.
Anon., Jr. (British Division)

PARSLEY. A chef's idea of decor.

PARTISAN. A voter with a rifle.

PARTY. Something a hostess wishes she had not given.
Oscar Wilde

PAS DE DEUX. Father of twins. *Anon., Jr. (British Division)*

PASS. A written permit to pan a show.

PASSÉ. The past tense, socially.

PASSENGERS. Shock absorbers on buses.
Changing Times, The Kiplinger Magazine

PASSION. Perpetual emotion.   Anon.

PASSPORT PICTURE. A photo of a man that he can laugh at
without realizing that it looks exactly the way his friends
see him.   Boston Herald

PASSWORD. A vocal key.

PATENT PENDING. "Hands off till we can get rid of some more
stock."

PATHOLOGIST. A doctor who invents diseases for other doctors
to cure.   Judge

PATIENCE. An infinite capacity for being pained.
— Being able to wait for the first coat of paint to dry before
adding the second.   Marcelene Cox
— The ability to idle your motor when you feel like stripping
your gears.   Howard W. Newton
— The quality that is needed most just as it is exhausted.
Carey MacWilliams
— The virtue of those who lack courage and strength.
Christina of Sweden

PATIENT. Symptoms with relatives attached.   Anon. nurse

PATRIARCH. An ancient man who is too old for Santa Claus
and too young for God.

PATRIOTISM. Geographic loyalty.
— Looking out for yourself by looking out for your country.
Calvin Coolidge
— Your conviction that this country is superior to all other
countries because you were born in it.
George Bernard Shaw

— Self-interest multiplied by population.   *Anon.*
— The last resort of a scoundrel.   *Dr. Samuel Johnson*
— The first resort of a scoundrel.   *Ambrose Bierce*

PATRON. A customer who doesn't ask prices.
  PATRONESS. A patronizing lady.

PATTI, ADELINA. A tiny woman in a bright orange wig who,
  late in life, sounded like a bicycle pump.   *Igor Stravinsky*

PAUNCH. A bulging trunk.
— A blow struck with the fist.   *Charlestonese*

PAUPER. The guy vot married Mommer.
                              Dartmouth *Jack O'Lantern*

PAWN. To leave a purchase as a deposit on cash.
  PAWNBROKER. One who lives off the flat of the land.
                                          Lionel Shelly
    — A man who takes an interest in things.   *Fred Allen*

PAX IN BELLO. Freedom from indigestion.   *Anon., Jr.*

PEACE. Time out.   *Leo C. Rosten*
— The white space between the chapters in the history books.
— The shortest distance between two wars.
  PEACE TREATY. An agreement setting forth the basis for
    the next war.

PEAR. A banana with the girdle off.   *Charlie McCarthy*

PEASANT. A hillbilly that can't speak English.

PEDAGOGUE. A place where Jews worship.   *Anon., Jr.*
— An animal with large ears.   *Anon., Jr.*

PEDANT. A person suffering from first-degree knowledge.
  PEDANTRY. Shiny pants acquired at a seat of learning.
    — Pride in the way you walk.   *Anon., Jr.*

PEDESTRIAN. A man whose son is home from college.
                                          American Boy

— A man who has two cars, a wife, and a son in high school.
Leatherneck

— A man with a wife and three grown daughters. *Jan Murray*

— A creature whose nerves are stronger than my brakes.
Ruth K. Levinson*

— A car owner who has found a parking space.
Hawley R. Everhart

— One who always has the right of way—to the hospital.

— Two classes: The quick and the dead. *Anon.*

PEDIGREE. The bark of a family tree.

PEEP. A sneak peek.
    PEEPHOLE. More than one poison.   *New Yorkese*
    PEEPING TOM. A window shopper.   *Don Quinn**

— A student of anatomy.

— A Doubting Thomas who wants to be convinced.
Anon. psychiatrist

— A guy who spends his time in the inside looking out for
standing on the outside looking in.
Capt. Billy's Whiz Bang

    PEEP SHOW. A dirty look.   *Don Quinn**

PEGLER, WESTBROOK. A man born with a hangover.
H. Allen Smith

PEKINESE. A cross between a muff and a chrysanthemum.
Alexander Woollcott

PENALTY. The price of something that wasn't for sale.

PENELOPE. The last hardship that Ulysses endured on his
journey.   *Anon., Jr.*

PENINSULA. A neck of land constantly washed by water.
Anon., Jr.

PENITENCE. The remorse code.

PENITENTIARY. A mugg's monastery.   *Leonard Neubauer**

PENSION. Pay given to a state hireling for treason to his
country.   *Dr. Samuel Johnson*

PENTHOUSE. A bad place for a good girl.

Arthur Somers Roche

— And vice versa.

PENURY. The wages of the pen.   *Anon. novelist*

PEOPLE. The plural of me.
— Animals who want to be different.

PERAMBULATOR. A vehicle to air the son, or vice versa.

Dr. S. B. Harding

PERFECT TIMING. Being able to turn off the "hot" and "cold" shower faucets at the same time.   *Karen Chandler*

PERFECTION. Such a nuisance that I often regret having cured myself of using tobacco.   *Emile Zola*

PERFUME. Any smell that is used to drown a worse one.

Elbert Hubbard

PERHAPS. The calling card of hope.   *Albert A. Brandt*

PERIOD. A dot at the end of a sentence. Period costumes are dresses all covered with dots.   *Anon., Jr.*

PERJURER. A person who testifies in court.

PERMANENT WAVE. A kink for a day.   *Anon.*

PERSONAL APPEARANCE. An adventure by a picture player to discover if he is loved by others, too.

PERSONALITY. The ability to get along with banana oil instead of elbow grease.   Pensacola *Gosport*

PESSIMIST. A man who tells the truth prematurely.   *Cyrano*
— A man who is never happy unless he is miserable, and even then he is not pleased. *Anon., Jr. (British Division)*
— A man who thinks everyone is as nasty as himself and hates them for it.   *George Bernard Shaw*
— A fellow who lives with an optimist.   *College Humor*

— A guy who feels bad when he feels good for fear he'll feel worse when he feels better. *Ted Robinson*

— One who says things are going to get worse.

OPTIMIST. One who says things couldn't get any worse.

Anon.

— One who believes that all women are bad.

OPTIMIST. One who hopes so. *Julius Tannen**

— One who makes difficulties of his opportunities.

OPTIMIST. One who makes opportunities of his difficulties.

Vice Admiral Mansell, R.N.

— A man who is afraid women's necklines will go higher this year.

OPTIMIST. One who buys a pair of elevator shoes.

— A cured optimist.

PETITION. A list of people who didn't have the nerve to say "no." *The Sign*

— A sucker list.

PETRIFIED FOREST. A bunch of trees that came up the hard way.

PETROLEUM. What you cover floors with.

Anon., Jr. (British Division)

PETTICOAT. A slip that does.

PETTING. Blind youth fumbling for happiness.

— A study of anatomy in Braille. *Ava Gardner*

PH.D. THESIS. Transferring bones from one graveyard to another. *J. Frank Dobie*

PHARMACIST. A man in a white coat who stands behind the soda counter selling dollar watches in a drugstore. *Anon.*

PHILADELPHIA. The City of Brotherly Loot.

Marquis Childs & John C. Turner

PHILANDERER. A person who gives money freely to charitable and needy institutions. *Anon., Jr.*

PHILANDERING. Amorous philanthropy.

PHILANTHROPIST. A bandit who is kind to beggars.
— The richest man in the cemetery. *Ed Wynn*
— One who has the power of throwing his voice. *Anon., Jr.*
  PHILANTHROPY. The refuge of people who wish to annoy
  their fellow creatures. *Oscar Wilde*
  — Paying Paul.

PHILATELIST. One who loves postage stamps for their own
sake.

PHILISTINES. Inhabitants of the Philippine Islands. *Anon., Jr.*

PHILOSOPHER. A forsooth-sayer.
— A person who always knows what to do until it happens
to him. *Anon.*
  PHILOSOPHY. The ability to bear with calmness the mis-
  fortunes of our friends. *French proverb*
  — The system of being unhappy intelligently.
  The Traveler
  — The common sense of the next century.
  Henry Ward Beecher
  — Like a pigeon, something to be admired as long as it
  isn't over your head. *Anon.*
  — Unintelligible answers to insoluble problems. *F.P.A.*
  — One philosopher arguing that all others are jackasses.
  He usually proves it, and I should add that he usually
  proves that he is one himself. *H. L. Mencken*
  — When he who hears doesn't know what he who speaks
  means, and when he who speaks doesn't know what he
  himself means—that's philosophy. *Anon.*
  — What you didn't know. *Bertrand Russell*
  SCIENCE. What you know. *Ibid.*

PHONOGRAPH RECORD. A speaking likeness.

PHOTO. "I know that a photograph attempts to lend perma-
nence to what is originally a transitory visual experience.
A photograph is a reproduction of something actually seen.
I know that photographs are flat, printed on paper, and

completely intangible. I know that light and shadow are imprinted in the form of lines, curves, and circle outlines which, by visual association, translate into an infinite variety of shapes and forms. I know that clarity, mood, degree of animation, and subtlety of detail vary with the skill, technique, and discernment of the photographer. Since I have not been able to see since I was two years old, I have virtually no visual recollection."   *Rose Resnick*

PHOTOGRAPHER. A reporter with his brains knocked out.
Anon. reporter

MODERN PHOTOGRAPHER. A man who thinks the hippopotamus's tonsils are more beautiful than Whistler's Mother.   *M. F. Agha*

TRICK PHOTOGRAPHY. Focus pocus.

PHYSICAL EDUCATION. What a young boy gets each time he goes to the beach.   *Hal Holbrook*

PHYSICIAN. He who collects when God has cured.
Spanish proverb
— A man who pours drugs of which he knows little into a body of which he knows less.   *Voltaire*

PIANO. A harp with hammers.
PLAYER PIANO. Henry Ford's conception of Paderewski.
PIANIST. A handworker hammering at a horizontal harp.
Anon.

PICKPOCKET. A man who believes that every crowd has a silver lining.   *Leonard Neubauer**

PICNIC. An ant's lunch.

PICTURE WINDOW. One you can't open.   *William V. Shannon*

PICTURESQUE. Old, but too pretty to be torn down.

PIDGIN. The English language pitched in the key of Asia.

PIE CRUST. Custard coffin.   *Shakespeare*

PIER. A disappointed bridge.   *James Joyce*

PIG. A hog's little boy. *Anon., Jr.*

PILGRIMAGE. A long trip to visit someone who isn't there.

PILLOW. Headquarters. *Cynic's Cyclopaedia*

PIMP. A public relations man for a private relations girl.

PINEAPPLE. The porcupine of the palm family.

PINTO. A sport model horse.

PIONEER. A man who can remember when he could have bought half of Main Street for $100.
— A man who could run faster than the Indians.

PIRACY. Commerce without manners.
  PIRATE. A robber with a boat.
  — A salt-water thief. Shakespeare, *Twelfth Night*
  — A briny burglar.

PITFALL. The space between the good intentions that the road to hell is paved with.

PITTSBURGH. Hell with the lid off. *Anon.*
— A city in Pennsylvania where they manufacture iron and steal. *Anon., Jr.*

PLAGIARISM. The only "ism" in which Hollywood believes.
Dorothy Parker
— Stealing a ride on someone else's train of thought.
Russell E. Curran
— Taking something from one man and making it worse.
George Moore
  PLAGIARIST. One who gives birth to an adopted baby.
Anon.
  — A literary body-snatcher.
  — A writer of plays. *Anon., Jr.*
  PLAGIARISTS. All the makers of dictionaries. *Voltaire*
  PLAGIARIZE. To take the thought or style of another whom one has never, never read.*

---

* Possibly by Ambrose Bierce.

PLANET. A body of earth surrounded by sky.   *Anon., Jr.*

PLANNING. The art of putting off until tomorrow what you have no intention of doing today.

PLATITUDE. A remark that is too true to be good.

PLATONIC. Play for one, tonic for the other.   *Marie Brewer*
PLATONIC FRIENDSHIP. One that half the town says isn't.
                                                   Raymond Duncan
PLATONIC LOVE. Sex above the ears. *Thyra Samter Winslow*
PLATONICISM. A type of love once affected by women who feared mustaches were contagious.

PLAYBOY. A plowboy with a Rolls-Royce.
— A painter of towns.

PLEASURE. The reward of anticipation and the threshold of disappointment.
— A cheap substitute for happiness.

PLEBISCITE. An election in No Man's Land.
— The chief disease affecting the veins.
                                   Anon., Jr. (British Division)

PLUMBER. A fellow who gets paid for sleeping under other people's sinks.   *Anon.*
— An adventurer who traces leaky pipes to their source.
                                          Arthur "Bugs" Baer
CONCEITED PLUMBER. One who'll look at Niagara Falls and say, "Give me time and I could fix it."   *Meyer Davis*

PLUM PUDDING. Fruit cake with a hotfoot.

PNEUMONIA (Hollywood). A cold with a press gent.
                                                   Al Rosen
POACHER. A tramp in the woods.

POCKET. A built-in mitten.

POEM. An extravagance you hope to get away with.
                                                   Robert Frost

POET. A nightingale, who sits in darkness and sings to cheer its own solitude with sweet sounds.

Percy Bysshe Shelley

— A juggler of words.

— Something that can't go to bed without making a song about it. *Dorothy L. Sayers*

— To transfer a liquid, i.e., "Poet from the pitcher to the glass." *Charlestonese*

POETIC LICENSE. Byron. Yale *Record*

— A license you get from the Post Office to keep poets. You get one also if you want to keep a dog. It costs two dollars and you call it a dog license. *Anon., Jr.*

POETRY. Faith. *Ralph Waldo Emerson*

— Music. *Richard E. Burton*

— Language singing to itself.

— Truth in its Sunday clothes. *Joseph Roux*

— The best words in the best order. *Samuel T. Coleridge*

— The spontaneous overflow of powerful feelings: it takes its origin from emotion recollected in tranquillity.

William Wordsworth

— Imaginary gardens with real toads in them.

Marianne Moore

— A wonderful game with words.

Irene Welch Grisson, Poet Laureate of Idaho

— Blind painting. *Time* Magazine

— A form of expression for them and those
Who can't express themselves in prose. *Harry Ruby*

— Writing where every line begins with a capital letter.

Anon., Jr.

— A literary gift—chiefly because you can't sell it.

Cynic's Cyclopaedia

POISE. An acquired characteristic which enables a man to buy a new pair of shoes at the same time he is ignoring a hole in his sock.

— The art of raising the eyebrows instead of the roof.
                                        Howard W. Newton
— The ability to face the guillotine without losing your head.
                                        Anon.

POLECAT. A small animal with an overdeveloped defense mechanism.

POLICE. Men fully able to meet and compete with criminals.
                                        Mayor John F. Hylan
POLICE REPORTER. A reporter who knows a policeman.

POLITENESS. A form of behavior often mistaken for good manners.   *Harry Ruby*
— Offering your seat to a lady when you get off a crowded bus.   *Lone Star Scanner*
— Not speaking evil of people with whom you have just dined until you are at least a hundred yards from their house.
                                        André Maurois
— One half good nature and the other half good lying.
                                        Mary Wilson Little
— A pleasing way to get nowhere with women.

POLITICS. The art of making possible that which is necessary.
                                        Paul Valéry
— The highly ceramic art of molding scum to your own desires.   *Francis Leo Golden*
— The art of obtaining money from the rich and votes from the poor on the pretext of protecting each from the other.
                                        Oscar Ameringer
— The science of how who gets what, when and why.
                                        Sidney Hillman
— History in action.   *Roger Butterfield*
    POLITICAL APPOINTMENT. A job in which the work consists of getting the job.
    POLITICAL CAMPAIGN. A war in which everybody shoots from the lip.   *Raymond Moley*
    POLITICAL CONTRIBUTION. The life of the party.

POLITICAL ECONOMY. The science which teaches us to get the greatest benefit with the least possible amount of honest labour. *Anon., Jr. (British Division)*

POLITICAL PLATFORM. A stage constructed entirely of springboards.

POLITICAL SCIENCE. The science of interfering in public affairs. *Anon.*

POLITICIAN. A dealer in promises. *Gabriel Chevallier*
— A person who can talk in circles while standing four-square. *Changing Times*
— One who is willing to do anything on earth for the workers except become one. *Judge*
— A man who identifies the sound of his own voice with the infallible voice of the people.

Marquis Childs or
Joseph Kinsey Howard

— One who fools all of the people at election time.
— A dog whose bite is worse than his bark.
— A person with whose politics you don't agree. If you agree with him, he is a statesman. *David Lloyd George*
— A goon with the wind. *Bob Hope*
— One that would circumvent God.

Shakespeare
(*Hamlet*, Act V, Scene 1)

POLO. Ping-pong with ponies.
WATER POLO. A soggy version of soccer. The team whose pulmotor breaks down first is declared the loser.

POLONIUS. A mythical sausage. *Anon., Jr.*

POLYANDRY. Every woman needs five husbands: an intellectual companion, a muscular toiler, a financial genius, a romantic playboy, and a practical plumber.
The Gas Flame

POLYGAMY. Every man needs five wives: a movie sweetheart, an English valet, a hotel chef, an attentive audience, and a trained nurse. *The Gas Flame*

— A marriage system under which a man has all his wives at the same time.
— A system where the wives fight each other instead of their husband. *Anon.*

Polygon. A dead parrot. *Anon., Jr. (British Division)*

Ponder. To lay an egg thoughtfully.

Pontificate. To talk like a stuffed shirt.

Pop. What happens when you wet a Rice Krispie.

Popcorn. The corn the audience eats.

Pope, Headgear Helen. An oily American rider.
New Yorkese

Popularity. The small change of glory. *French proverb*
— A pleasant visitor who always leaves in the morning.
Sour Owl

Population. People considered as statistics.

Pornography. Bedridden literature.

Portfolio. A long brief case.

Positive. Being wrong at the top of your voice.
Ambrose Bierce

Possession. (by spirits) Feeling like the devil. *Anon., Jr.*
possessiveness. The revenge of the possessed.

Possibly. No, in three syllables.

Posterity. What happens when you try to get monkeys to stand up straight. *Anon., Jr.*

Postman. A reader of postcards.

Post Office. The old stamping grounds. *Fibber McGee*

POSTHUMOUS. A child born after the death of its parents.
Anon., Jr.

POSTURE. What one does with the body when not thinking about it.

POTATO. An Irish avocado. *Fred Allen*

POUT. A pet expression.

POVERTY. The only thing wrong with the poor.
George Bernard Shaw
— No disgrace—but that's about all that can be said for it.
R. M. Tucker

POWDER ROOM. A hoity toidy.

PRACTICAL. Possible of commercial exploitation.
PRACTICAL JOKER. One who can get a private office and a big salary from a TV program in exchange for his gags.
PRACTICAL NURSE. One who marries a wealthy patient.

PRATTFALL. A humorous backdrop. *Don Quinn**

PRAYER. A little message to God, sent at night to get the cheaper rate. *Anon., Jr.*
— An appeal which must never be answered; if it is, it ceases to be prayer and becomes correspondence.
Oscar Wilde
— A declaration of dependence.

PRECEDENT. A footprint in the concrete of time.

PRECOCITY. An egg cackling.

PREJUDICE. An opinion that holds a man.
— A frame-up of mind.
— Being down on anything you're not up on. *Anon.**
— Not liking somebody before you've even met him.
Mike Hobson
— The divine right of fools.
— The only luxury left to the poor. *Douglas Churchill**

PRESIDENT. Yes-man to the majority.
EX-PRESIDENT. A hibernating messiah. *Walter Lippmann*

PRESS. A piece of machinery used to give rumor the appearance of impeachability.
— The mouth-organ of the people.   *Anon., Jr.*
  PRESS AGENT. One who takes in lying for a living.
  — A guy who hitched his braggin' to a star.   *Jim Caye*
  — That which, if you don't have, no one will read about things you didn't say.   *Paul Gray*

PRETZEL. A biscuit on a bender.

PREVIEW. A clambake in Technicolor.   *Morton Thompson*
— A place where four or five men, making four or five thousand a week, go to watch a pimply-faced kid write "It stinks" on a card.   *Nunnally Johnson*
— The beginning of a studio shake-up.   *Groucho Marx*

PRICES. Materials, wages, taxes, profits added up and divided by customers.

PRINCESS. An accident that occurred in the attempt to create a prince.   *Manfred Gottfried*

PRINCIPLES. Prejudices, whitewashed and surmounted by a neon halo.   *Anon.*

PRINTING. The angles and curves used to convey or obscure ideas.
— An embalming process for thoughts.
— An invention that makes an ear out of an eye.
— The greatest misfortune that ever befell man.   *Disraeli*

PRISM. A place where convex are kept.   *Anon.*

PRISON. A hostelry where the guest is always wrong.
                    Warden James A. Johnston, Alcatraz Island
— The tuition you pay to learn you can't sell anything that isn't yours.
— A school to which criminals are sent to figure out their mistakes.
— The last resort of a scoundrel.

PRISONER. A bird in a guilty cage.   *Molly McGee*
— One who has committed the crime of getting caught.

PROCESSED CHEESE. Solidified floor wax. The triumph of technology over conscience. *Clifton Fadiman*

PROCLAMATION. A greeting card to a nation.

PROCRASTINATION. The art of keeping up with yesterday.
Don Marquis

PRODIGY. A child who is just as smart at four as he will be at forty. *Marianne*

PRODUCER, HOLLYWOOD. A man who won't take no for an answer.
— A man who knows what he wants but can't spell it.
Shakespeare
— A man who doesn't know what he wants and wouldn't like it if he got it. *Bacon*
— An executive who wears a worried look on his assistant's face.
— An ulcer with authority. *Fred Allen*
— A man who has got hold of some money and some brains, and is using the money.
— A fellow who found it more profitable to sell ham on film than ham on rye. *Bert Lytell*
— A person who gets too much credit if a show is good and too much blame if it's bad. *Fred Coe*
ASSOCIATE PRODUCER. About the only guy in Hollywood who will associate with a producer. *Fred Allen*

PROFANITY. A meaningless use of words which allows the speaker to vocalize and exercise his tone code. Since he has reached the linguistic stage of development he swears. Otherwise he would coo. *Prof. Kenneth Bartlett*
— The father tongue. *Harry Martin°*

PROFESSIONAL. An amateur who has decided to eat regularly.
PROFESSIONAL TENNIS PLAYER. One who reports his income.
Jimmy Cannon

PROFESSOR. One who talks in someone else's sleep.
W. H. Auden

PROFESSORS. There are two types: the dead and the buried.
Anon. collegiate

PROFIT. Wages for those who didn't work.
PROFITEERING. The fortunes of war.

PROGRESS. The continuing effort to make things we eat, drink, and wear as good as we think they used to be.
Buffalo *Evening News*
— A state of human development when a man pays a laundry to destroy his shirts. San Diego *Aztec*
— The exchange of one nuisance for another. *Havelock Ellis*
— Making different mistakes.
— A movement forward based on a universal innate desire on the part of every organism to live beyond its income.
Samuel Butler

PROHIBITION. A political program that raised the toxic immunity of America 87.3 per cent in 14 years.

PROMINENCE. Having the lowest license number in town.

PROMISE. The soul of an advertisement. *Dr. Johnson*

PROMISSORY NOTE. A nervous breakdown on paper. *Anon.*

PROMOTOR. A bust developer.

PROPAGANDA. The other side's case put so convincingly that it annoys you.
— A lie told to a million people.

PROPER BOSTONIAN. A person who didn't just happen; he was planned. *Cleveland Amory*

PROPERTY. A sacred trust expressly granted by God, the Bible, and the Recorder's Office. *Leo C. Rosten*

PROPHET. A man who foresees trouble. *Mr. Dooley*

PROPHYLACTIC. To bear young in large numbers—a rabbit is said to be prophylactic.   *Anon., Jr.*

PROPOSITION. A pregnant question.

PROSELYTE. A woman of the streets.   *Vassar Senior*

PROSPECTUS. A man who finds gold.
                    Anon., Jr. (British Division)

PROSTITUTE. A busy body.   *Anon.*
— A mistress on a piecework basis.

PROTESTANT. A woman who gets her living through an immortal life.   *Anon., Jr.*

PROUD. Loving oneself dearly.

PROVIDENCE. Angels rushing in where fools fear to tread.

PRUDE. A virtuous exhibitionist.
— A woman that wears two-inch straps on her bathing suit.
                    Missouri Outlaw
— A native of Boston.   *Foolish Dictionary*

PRUNE. A plum that has seen better days.
                    Foolish Dictionary

PSEUDONYM. The state or condition a poet gets into just before writing.   *Anon., Jr.*

PSYCHIATRIST. A man who has been trained to understand and explain to other people the facts of life—which he himself has to avoid in order to become a psychiatrist.
— A man who goes to the Folies Bergère and looks at the audience.   *Dr. Mervyn Stockwood*
— A doctor with moneyed patients who helps them live with it.
— Someone who'll listen to you as long as you don't make sense.   *Maxwell Hyman*
— A doctor who doesn't have to worry so long as other people do.

— A doctor who can't stand the sight of blood. *Joe Cohen*

— A Freud egg. *Leonard Neubauer*

PSYCHIATRISTS. People with the same problems as anyone else, but with an accent. *Stella Adler*

PSYCHIATRY. The troubled science. *R. H. Berg*

— The only business where the customer is always wrong.

— A terrible waste of couches. *Rosina Pagan*

PSYCHOLOGY. A word rung in to distract attention when the explaining gets difficult. Boston *Transcript*

CHILD PSYCHOLOGY. What children manage parents with.
Mrs. Richard Fisher

PTERODACTYL. The early bird.

PTOLEMY. A Greek scientist who discovered the cause of ptomaine poisoning. *Anon., Jr.*

PUB-CRAWLING. An irregular movement from bar to bar, like syncopation. *Anon.*

PUBERTY. The awkward age when a child is too old to say something cute and too young to say something sensible.
Anon.

— The dawn of creation.

PUBLIC. One immense ass. *Horace Greeley*

— A scurvy master. *Italian proverb*

— The people who pay the taxes and buy the goods and better damn well keep their noses out of politics and the way business is run.

PUBLIC RELATIONS. Press agentry on a yearly basis.

PUBLIC RELATIONS COUNSELOR. A press agent with a manicure. *Alan Gordon*

— A press agent with two telephones.
Madison Avenue executive

PUBLICITY. The art of putting the best feat forward. *N. W.*

PUBLISHER. A smart merchant who takes a block of spruce, slices it into 500 sheets, sprays ink on it, and sells it at $5 a copy.

PUCK. A hard rubber disk that hockey players strike when they can't hit one another. *Jimmy Cannon*

PUERILITY. The state of being pure, like virginity, although puerility does not necessarily indicate virginity. *Anon., Jr.*

PUGILIST. A boxer with an education.

PUN. A joke based on the infirmities of a language.
— Language on vacation.
Christopher Morley, says Clifton Fadiman
— The lowest form of humor—when you don't think of it first. *Oscar Levant*

PUNCTUALITY. The ability to guess to the minute exactly how late a girl will be for an appointment. *Vittorio de Sica*
— The art of arriving for an appointment just in time to be indignant at the tardiness of the other party.
Liverpool *Echo*
— The thief of time. *Oscar Wilde*

PUNISHMENT. Preventive pain.

PUNCTURE. A hissing sound followed by profanity. *Judge*

PURGATORY. The Ellis Island of Hell.
— A place where those go who are too good to go to heaven and too bad to go to hell. *Anon., Jr.*

PURITAN. One who hangs his cat on Monday for killing a mouse on Sunday.
PURITANISM. The haunting fear that someone, somewhere, may be happy. *H. L. Mencken*

PYRAMIDS. A range of mountains between France and Spain.
Anon., Jr.

PYORRHEA. The seaport of Athens. *Ibid.*

Q

Q. There really isn't much to be said for Q without raising the voice, as everyone knows who has tried to find one in gold paper to paste in a new hat, or in embroidery to sew on a shirtsleeve. Not that this is a particularly apt illustration of Q's inutility, inasmuch as few people whose names open with a Q ever have new hats or shirts worth embroidering.

Q is number 17 in the line-up, and seventeen is the awkward age. Q isn't what I'd call one of our Belliest Lettres. As a matter of fact, it is a sneer letter. It cannot be pronounced without a twitch of the nostrils and a supercilious twist of the mustache. You can't be a Q-man and keep a stiff upper lip.

The old Romans probably found the greatest use for Q, and among certain of the Latin peoples it still enjoys some usage, particularly in connection with some of the dumber colloquialisms (Good God, it's even in the middle of *that!*) such as *¿Quién sabe?* and *Quo vadis?*—meaning "Who knows?" and "Who the hell cares?", respectively. Now that Latin is a defunct language, Q may find its well-deserved way to the dead letter office.

In any case, you may take it from one who has lived with it, Q is the stepchild of the alphabet. It hasn't the exotic zip of Z or the sweet mystery of X. It's just eccentric without being interesting. Q is a philological mistake; a G with its mouth shut, an O with a hangover. As Quidnunc Quimby so well says in his *Kiddies' Hornbook*:

> Q can be found
>   With his tongue out to here,
> Giving P the cold shoulder,
>   And R the Bronx cheer.

*Don Quinn**

189

QUACK. A wolf with a sheepskin.

QUAKER. A man who loves his neighbor's life.

QUARANTINE. A concentration camp for germs.
— A four-masted ship.   *Anon., Jr.*

QUEEN. A king's best friend and severest critic.
   QUEEN ELIZABETH. The feminine of drake.
                                    Anon., Jr. (British Division)
   QUEEN VICTORIA. The heiress of a whole series of question-
   able successions.   *Tony Mayer*
— The only queen who sat on a thorn for sixty-three years.
                                                Anon., Jr.

QUEER. Unfamiliar (thank God!)   *Don Quinn* *

QUEUE. A train of people.   *Anon., Jr.*

QUICKIE. A motion picture shot at sunrise.

QUIET. Noise you don't mind.

QUININE. The bark of a tree: canine is the bark of a dog.
                                                Anon., Jr.
— The bark that is better than its bite.

QUIXOTE, DON. The good night to knights.

QUIZ. Pranks for the memory.

QUOTATION. Something that somebody said that seemed to
   make sense at the time.

R

R.   The main thing about the letter R is that without it you couldn't eat oysters. If you couldn't eat oysters, there would be no pearls and no ptomaine poisoning. That would do away with the letter P, and virtually disrupt the whole alphabet. If you disrupted the alphabet, chaos would result. How would you look up a telephone number? How would you go to the dictionary? There wouldn't be any dictionaries at all, right-handed, left-handed, or ambidextrous. There wouldn't be anything. God would have to start right in again and make the world over in six days.

That, incidentally, is the trouble with the world. It was turned out in six days—a quickie. It needed more thought. I'm not suggesting another Director, but I think He could have got a better cast. And I'm not so sure the script was right, either. I'm not saying that the script wasn't artistic. It has grim tragedy, and ruthlessness, and poverty, and war, and hatred, and dictators—proletarian and fascistic—and unemployment, and all the other things that make a world exciting. But it's not my stuff.

I like to read about such things occasionally, but when it comes to living, I like the Happy Ending. I'd like a world where democracy was really safe, safer even than oysters in the months with the letter R in them.

Then the world could be my oyster. And yours, too.

*Morrie Ryskind**

— The canine letter, because it is uttered with some resemblance to the growl or snarl of a cur.

Dr. Samuel Johnson

RABID FAN. A guy who boos a television set.   *Jimmy Cannon*

RACE. Two or more persons who see some difference between themselves and other people.

RACE SUICIDE. The tendency to have more fun and less children.

RACE TRACK. Where the windows clean the people.

Earl Wilson

RACKETEERING. Big Business on a small scale.

RADICAL. A conservative out of a job.

Richmond *News Leader*

— One who wants to tackle all evil at the root.

Boiled down from 5,000 words by Dwight MacDonald

— A man with both feet firmly planted in the air.

Franklin D. Roosevelt

RADIO. A toy to tickle the ears of fools.　　*Francis Beeding*

— A conduit through which prefabricated din can flow into our homes.　　*Aldous Huxley*

— A device which permits speakers to state without fear of contradiction.

— A repercussion instrument.

— An instrument perfectly suited to a prison.　　*Leon Trotsky*

— The box-that-talks-too-loud.　　*Anon. Indian*

RADIO ADVERTISING. Persuasion by vibration.

RADIO COMMERCIAL. A signal to shut off the radio.

RAFFLE. A scheme that gives you a chance to get nothing for something.　　*Cynic's Cyclopaedia*

RAINBOW. Heaven's promise in Technicolor.　　*Anon.*

RAINFALL. The chief product of the Hawaiian Islands.

Anon., Jr.

RAISE HEARSE. An animal that comes in last when you bat him.　　*New Yorkese*

RAISIN. A prune whipped down to a nub.　　*Blue Gate*

RANCH. Something you find between two Good Humor men.

Red Skelton

RANK. A great beautifier.
> *Sir Edward George Earle Lytton Bulwer Lytton, baron*

RAPE. A hit & run romance.
— Seduction minus sales talk. *Morton Thompson*°
— Assault with intent to please. *Anon.*
  STATUTORY RAPE. When a man is seduced by a girl under
  twenty. *Tennessee Williams*

RAPIDS. An escalator in a river.

RATIONING. Less and less of more and more, often and oftener.
> Arcadia (Wis.) *News-Letter*

RATTLETRAP. Last year's model.

RAZOR BLADE. Something you look for while the lather dries.
> *Anon.*

REACTIONARY. A somnambulist walking backwards.
> *Franklin D. Roosevelt*
— A person who sits in his easy chair on Sunday, never
thinking that tomorrow is Monday, but only that yesterday
was Saturday. *Ferdinand Pecora*

READERS. There are two sorts: one who carefully goes through
a book, and the other who as carefully lets the book go
through him. *Douglas Jerrold*

READING. A nervous habit to avoid thinking.
— Thinking with someone else's head instead of one's own.
> *Schopenhauer*

REAL ESTATE. The ground you can keep other people off of.

REALIST. One who insists on touching wet paint signs.
> *Leonard Neubauer*°

REAR ADMIRALS. Very low types of admirals. *Anon., Jr.*

REBATE. Putting another worm on the hook. *Ibid.*

REBUTTAL. Being knocked down twice by the same goat.
Barney Glazer

RECALL. A way voters can change their minds, adopted with women's suffrage.

RECEIVER. An official appointed by the court to take what's left. *Robert Frost*
RECEIVERSHIP. Business as usual during altercations.

RECESSIONAL. Exit music played when a religious show is over.

RECIPROCITY. Seconding the emotion. *Elbert Hubbard*

RECKLESS DRIVER. One who passes you on the highway in spite of all you can do. *Lincoln Parker*

REDDISH. A vegetable with a sharp taste and an ability to reincarnate itself for hours and hours. *New Yorkese*

RED INK. In the ketchup. *Dan Parker*

RED FLAG. A banner to infuriate bulls and property holders.

RED LIGHT. The place where you catch up with the motorist who passed you at 60 m.p.h. a mile back.
Robert Q. Lewis

REDECORATE. To refurnish, repaper, repaint, and repent.
Dorothy Gulman*

REEFS. What you put on coffins. *Anon., Jr. (British Division)*

REFINEMENT. The ability to yawn without opening your mouth. *Anon.*

REFORMER. One who raises eyebrows for a living.
— One who insists upon his conscience being your guide.
Milard Miller
— One who is trying to make the world a better place to die in.

— One who, when he smells a rat, is eager to let the cat out of the bag.   *Foolish Dictionary*

— A guy who rides through a sewer in a glass-bottom boat.
Mayor James J. Walker

REFORMATORY. A repent house.

REFUGEE. The man who blows the whistle at a football game.
Anon., Jr.

— A fugitive from injustice.

REFUGEES. People who vote with their feet.
Berliner Illustrierte

REGRET. A feeling of loss for something never possessed.

— An appalling waste of energy; you can't build on it; it's only good for wallowing in.   *Katherine Mansfield*

REINCARNATION. A split infinity.   *Leonard Neubauer**

REINDEER. Horses with hatracks.   *Anon.*

RELATIONS. A tedious pack of people who haven't got the remotest knowledge of how to live nor the smallest instinct about when to die.   *Oscar Wilde*

RELATIVE. A natural enemy.   *Harry Hirshfield**

DISTANT RELATIVE. An uncle who recently borrowed money from you.   *Earl Wilson's column*

RICH RELATIVE. A wealthy ex-husband.   *Victor Borge*

RELIGION. Trust.

— Aspirin for perplexity.   *Jackson Parks**

— Faith in a problem to which the Lord only knows the answer.

—What the individual does with his own solitude. (If you are never solitary, you are never religious.)   *Dean Inge*

— The highest form of self-deception.

— Organized superstition.

— A substitute for fear.

— The prophet system.

— The alcohol of the soul.   *Robert Hume*

RELUCTANCE. A wisp o' the will.

REMARK. (Chance) Anything a man gets to say when two
women are talking. *Quote*

REMORSE. The price of a good time.
— Rats in the belfry.
— Beholding heaven and feeling hell. *George Moore*

RENDEZVOUS. A dated date.

RENO. The only place in the world where a judge frees a
guy for bad behavior. *Wilkie Mahoney*
— The largest inland seaport in America, with the tied running in and the untied running out. *Anon.*

RENT. The sum you pay the landlord for the privilege of
complaining. *R. C. O'Brien*

REPARTEE. A duel fought with the points of jokes.
Max Eastman
— Any reply that is so clever that it makes the listener wish
he had said it himself. *Elbert Hubbard*
— A clever reply a man thinks up on his way home after a
party. *Anon.*
— A remark that is better never than late. *Anon.*

REPENTANCE. A truce with sin.

REPRIEVE. A miscarriage of mercy. *Cynic's Cyclopaedia*
— Skipping the rope.

REPRIMAND. The reverse of the medal.

REPROBATE. One whose reputation bars probation.

REPUBLIC. A place where nobody can do anything in private.
Anon., Jr.
CONSERVATIVE REPUBLICAN. One who doesn't believe any-
thing new should ever be tried for the first time.
Mort Sahl

LIBERAL REPUBLICAN. One who does believe something should be tried for the first time but not now. *Ibid.*

REPUTATION. What others are not thinking of you.
Tom Masson

REQUIEM. Music played for those who can no longer hear.
— A mass meeting of the dead in a Catholic Church.
Anon., Jr.

RESEARCH. Eliminating the ninety-nine wrong ways of doing or seeing it.
APPLIED RESEARCH. Scientific activity dedicated to discovering gimcracks that magnetize green-backed paper.
Russell Baker
BASIC RESEARCH. Scientific activity dedicated to discovering what makes grass green. *Ibid.*

RESORT. A place where one commutes with nature.
— A place where girls wear their baiting suits. *Anon.*
— A hotel where no one knows how unimportant you are at home. *Anon.*

RESPECTABILITY. Public acclaim, the reward of scoundrels.
Bertrand Russell

RESPIRATION. The art of drawing breath.
— Composed of two acts, first inspiration and then expectoration. *Anon., Jr.*
— A handy thing to know how to do, especially if you live far from a doctor. *Ibid.*
ARTIFICIAL RESPIRATION. What you keep a man alive with when he is just dead. *Ibid.*

RESTAURANT. Where one goes to rest and rant. *Walt Lee*
— An institution for the distribution of indigestion.

RETRACTION. The revision of an insult to give it wider circulation.

RETREAT. A strategic maneuver by the army that is being licked.

REVENGE. Biting a dog because the dog bit you.
Austin O'Malley

REVIVAL. Religion with a vaudeville attachment.
Elbert Hubbard

REVOLT. A chain reaction to chains.

REVOLUTION. A complete renovation and reopening under new management.
— The quickest form of government.

REYNOLDS, DEBBIE. An angel with spurs. *Joseph Pasternak*

RHAPSODY. A testimonial written by a musical press agent.

RHETORIC. Language in a dress suit. *Foolish Dictionary*
— Fine talk!

RHUBARB. Bloodshot celery. *Anon.*

RHYME. One of the worst spelled words in the language.
Professor Skeat

RIALTO. The business end of Venus. *Anon., Jr.*

RICE. A building material largely used to fill up Chinks.
Don Quinn*

RICH. Money-stricken.
    RICH MAN. One who isn't afraid to ask the clerk to show him something cheaper. *Ladies' Home Journal*
    — The real outcast of society, and special missions should be organized for him. *Norman Macleod*
    RICHES. The wants you haven't got.

RIDING. The art of keeping a horse between yourself and the ground. *London Times*

RIDICULOUS. Too absurd to be funny.

RIGHTEOUS INDIGNATION. Your own wrath as compared to the shocking bad temper of others.   *Elbert Hubbard*

RIGOR MORTIS. The price of rigidity.   *Max Lerner*

RIN-TIN-TIN. A dog who hitched his waggin' to a star.   *Anon.*

RIOT. An emotional storm by a mob or a woman.
— Something made by two wrongs.   *Anon. collegiate*

RIPPLE. An apprentice Wave.   *Navy talk*

RIVER. A wet highway.

ROBBERY. Earning a living by doing unwanted work.

ROBERT BURNS. An epitaph for Robert Ingersoll.
    Henry Ward Beecher

ROBIN. A sparrow with high blood pressure.   *Matt Weinstock*

ROBINHOOD. To feel like a robin and hop around.   *Anon., Jr.*

ROCK 'N ROLL. The South's revenge for losing the Civil War.
— Defacing the music.
   ROCK 'N ROLL QUARTET. Four people who think the other three can't sing and are right.   *John Wingate*

ROD. A fish pole that costs more than $10.
    Dude's Dictionary

ROMANCE. Any other business but your own.
   ROMANTIC. A Roman being loyal to Rome.   *Anon., Jr.*

ROOF GARDEN. A café where you can be under the table and still up in the world.

ROOM TEMPERATURE. The place where they serve red wines.
    Anon.

ROOSEVELT, ELEANOR. Public Energy No. 1.

ROOSEVELT, THEODORE. A combination of St. Paul and St. Vitus.   *John Marley*

ROTARIAN. A man who serves his fellow men and can afford $2 for lunch.

ROTARY CLUB. An organization which admits only one of each kind, making it twice as exclusive as Noah's Ark.
Cynic's Cyclopaedia

ROUGE. That which makes a girl look nice when she doesn't use any. *College Humor*

ROUGH RIDERS. A regiment recruited from the aristocracy of the wild men of the west and the wild men of the aristocracy of the east. *O. Henry*

ROYAL MINT. What a king grows in his Palace Gardens.
Anon., Jr.

ROYALTY. A feather in a man's cap. *Oliver Cromwell*

RUDENESS. The reply we cannot think of.
New Statesman & Nation

RUG. A bedspread for people who sleep on the floor.
— $100 worth of tapestry to protect $10 worth of wood.
THROW RUG. A small rug that usually throws anyone who steps on it. *Margaret Schooley*

RUINS. Civilization's fallen arches.

RUM. An enclosed space within a building. *Charlestonese*

RUMBA. Waving good-bye without using your hands. *Anon.*
— A dance where the front of you goes along nice and smooth like a Cadillac and the back of you makes like a jeep.
Bob Hope's writers
— A dance in which one must keep a stiff upper hip.
— An asset to music. *Anon.*

RUMINANT. An animal that chews its cub. *Anon., Jr.*

RUMINATE. To think while digesting.

Russell, Bertrand. A foolish old man trying to be the keeper of our conscience.

Russia. A place where, if you don't want what you see, you're asking for it.
— A riddle wrapped in a mystery inside an enigma.

Sir Winston Churchill

Rut. A small grave.   *Ellen Glasgow*

S

S. In an all-star revue like this, S may be considered practically next-to-closing and, as such, in the most honored and envied position on the bill.

As master of ceremonies of the nineteenth letter in the alphabet, I don't have to do much barking to produce a sellout. All S acts are headliners. This is not because we're so good, but because there are so many of us we can afford to be choosy.

Almost any dictionary, filing cabinet, or sucker list will bulk largest under the letter S, and the Left-Handed Dictionary is no exception. Shakespeare and Shaw, sabotage and skyscrapers, seducers and self-denialists, shrouds and shysters, socialists and socialites—they're all here and all defined with twenty-first-century definitions.

You can't go wrong if, by chance, you open this dictionary on S and never leave here, and it's all right, too, if you work back from here, kosher fashion, to the beginning.

This is the section that has sex-appeal. It also has scoundrels, shoulder straps, silks, sins, sofas, and stenographers.

What more do you want from a serpentine letter hemmed in on one side by a rigid old reactionary better described, to avoid libel, as R—— and on the other by a toothless old Tory equally well described as T——?

Like the four seasons (described here as salt, pepper, mustard, and vinegar) you'll find everything under S. Stay as long as you like and if we have to go over to the B——'s for a bed, we can take it back and have the fun here—reading our heads off.   *Frank Scully**

— A letter that has in English the same hissing sound as in other languages, and unhappily prevails in so many of our words that it produces in the ear of a foreigner a continued sibilation. *Dr. Samuel Johnson*

S O S. A musical term meaning "same only softer." *Anon., Jr.*

Sables. The wages of sin. *Wisconsin Octopus*

Sabotage. Throwing a shoe for bad luck.

Sacrifice. A form of bargaining. *Holbrook Jackson*

Saddle. A chafing dish. *Irvin S. Cobb*
saddlebag. An equestrienne. *Anon.*

Sadist. Someone who is kind to masochists. *Vincent McHugh*

Saint. A man of convictions, who has been dead a hundred years, canonized now, but cannonaded while living.
H. L. Wayland
saint francis. Everybody's saint. *Reader's Digest*

Salesman. A priest in the temple of business.
super-salesman. One who can sell a double-breasted suit to a man with a Phi Beta Kappa key. *Anon.*
sales manager. The high priest of profits.
sales resistance. The triumph of mind over patter.
Boston *Transcript*

Saloon. An American institution that attempted to keep liquor from women. (Obsolete)

Samoa. The first stop to the left, after you leave San Francisco. *Robert Louis Stevenson*

San Francisco. A city with eleven months and several odd days of Indian Summer. *Charlie Groves*

Sandwich. Two slices of bread trying to get together.
club sandwich. A sandwich that fights back.

Sanhedrin. A Jewish virgin who went up to Jerusalem every year to be circumcised. *Anon., Jr.*

SANTA CLAUS. The fourth member of the Trinity.

SARDINE. A herring's pup.
                    Freddy James, The World's Worst Juggler

SARONG. A simple garment carrying the implicit promise that it will not long stay in place.   *E. B. White*

SATAN. The scarecrow in the religious cornfield.

SATELLITE. A stooge for a star.

SATIRE. A play that closes Saturday night. *George S. Kaufman*
SATIRIST. A worker in wrought irony.

SAUSAGE. Hash in cellophane pants.   *Anon.*

SAVAGES. People who don't know what is wrong until missionaries show them.   *Anon., Jr.*

SAVANT. A professor being quoted by a newspaper.

SAVINGS. Money that sleeps while you work.

SAVOIR FAIRE. Being a Boy Scout in society.
— The ability to smile when you discover your best pal and your best girl are both missing from the dance floor.
                    Keesler News
— The ability to keep talking until the other fellow picks up the check.   *Patuxent River Tester*

SCANDAL. Something that has to be bad to be good.   *Anon.*

SCENARIST. A man who intends to keep on writing until the producers learn to read.   *Harry Hirshfield**

SCHISM. Religion doing the split.

SCHOOL. A mental institution.

SCIENCE. A first-rate piece of furniture for a man's upper chamber if he has common sense on the ground floor.
                    Oliver Wendell Holmes

— The creation of dilemmas by the solution of mysteries.
— Material.
    religion. Immaterial.   *Anon., Jr. (British Division)*
    scientism. Making a noise like a scientist.
                          Dr. Margaret Mead
    scientist. A man who would rather count than guess.

Scotch. The executive's tranquilizer.   *John Beavan*
— Tight.
    scottish. Tighter.
    scotchman. A person whose thrift teaches him to take
      long steps to save shoe leather, but whose caution ad-
      vises him to take short steps to avoid ripping his pants.
                              Anon.
    scotch sunday drunk. A very unmanageable condition of
      spiritual ecstasy.   *Saturday Review*

Scoundrel. A man who won't stay bought.
             William Marcy ("Boss") Tweed

Scout. A fiend to all and a bother to every other scout.
                            Anon., Jr.

Scow. A floating hovel.

Scratch Sheet. A road map to the poorhouse.
                          Jimmy Cannon

Sculpture. Mud pies which endure.   *Cyril Connolly*
— An art that takes away superfluous material. *Michelangelo*

Sea. The fisherman's farm.   *Russian proverb*
    sea serpent. A nautical phenomenon that never appears
      when a first officer has a camera in his hand.
                           Russell Owen
    seabee. A soldier in a sailor's uniform, with Marine train-
      ing, doing civilian work at WPA wages.   *Anon. Seabee*
    seasickness. Traveling across the ocean by rail.
                           Ronny White

Seance. Sitting down with a few choice spirits.

SECRET. Something a woman tells everybody not to tell anybody. *Anon.*

SECRETARY. A stenographer who runs the boss.
PERFECT SECRETARY. One who can take down anything
that might come up. *Anon. boss*

SEDUCER. A bandit in the boudoir.
SEDUCTION. Education by demonstration.
— The perfect crime.

SEGREGATION. A Dixie malady.

SELF-DENIAL. The effect of prudence on rascality.
George Bernard Shaw

SELF-ESTEEM. The most voluble of the emotions.
Frank Colby

SELF-LOVE. The instrument of our preservation. *Voltaire*

SELF-POSSESSION. One of the very best of all earthly pos-
sessions. *George Prentice*
— The tenth point of the law. *Harry Thompson*

SELF-RESTRAINT. Feeling your oats without sowing them.
Shannon Fife

SEMANTICS. The art of telling a man you don't know what
he's talking about when you know very well what he's talking about but don't like what he's saying. *Charles Poore*

SEMINARY. A place where they bury the dead. *Anon., Jr.*

SENATE. A place where shirts are stuffed.
Leonard Neubauer°
— A club which a hundred men belong to but pay no dues.
Will Rogers
SENATOR. A creature that is half man and half horse.
Anon., Jr.

SENTENCE. A group of words starting with a subject and ending in a penitentiary.

SENTIMENT. The sediment of emotion.
SENTIMENTALITY. The use of ashes as a fuel.

SEPTUAGENARIAN. A man who makes the same mistakes he did at sixty.

SEPULCHER. Derived from "se" negative and "pulcher" fair. The place where beauty fades.
                                    Anon., Jr. (British Division)
SEQUEL. An author's second wind.

SERAGLIO. A light house.

SERENADE. The theme song of a seduction.
                                    Leonard Neubauer*
SERMON. A religious pep-talk.
                                    Rev. Dr. Frederic Sydney Fleming

SERVANT. One who does something for another for pay. Examples: parlormaids, parsons, physicians, Presidents, prostitutes.

SERVICE. The concept of doing something for nothing while doing someone for something.

SEWAGE CANAL. Something that connects the Mediterranean and the Red Sea.   *Anon., Jr.*

SEX. The formula by which one and one makes three.
— Something that children never discuss in the presence of their elders.   *Arthur Somers Roche*
— The lowest common denominator.   *Ted Taylor*
— The highest common denominator.
— The poor man's polo.   *Clifford Odets*

SEXAGENARIAN. One who no longer can enjoy it.   *Anon.*

SHAD. A lump of liver with a paper of pins stuck in it. *Anon.*

SHAKESPEARE. The sweet swan of Avon.   *Ben Jonson*
— A man whose writings are so excellent it is believed someone else must have written them.

— A savage with sparks of genius which shone in a dreadful darkness of night.   *Voltaire*
— A punning fool, bringing to the job far more enthusiasm than judgment.   *Clifton Fadiman*

Shampoo. Noodle soup.

Shavian. Unshaven.   *Don Quinn°*
    shavians. Cruel barbarians. The Shavs were a Russian race with a Spartan sense of humor.   *Anon., Jr.*

Shaving. What a man does to distinguish himself from the monkey.   *Anon.*
— A man's best excuse for admiring himself in the mirror.
                                                          Fred Beck
— Washing the face with a sword.

Shaw, George Bernard. The messenger boy of a new age.
                                              Marybeth Weinstein
— An old château not even haunted by a spirit.
                                              Maurice Maeterlinck
— A critic who has outlived the time for which he was born too soon.   Detroit *News*
— A wingless angel with an old maid's temperament.
                                              James G. Huneker
— A playwright who knew all of the answers, but none of the questions.   *Harold Hobson*

She. The objective of "he."   *Anon., Jr.*

Sheep. Mutton covered with wool.
                                  Anon., Jr. (British Division)
    sheepskin. Something presented to a college graduate to cover his intellectual nakedness.   *Robert M. Hutchins*

Shoddy. A small guy.   *New Yorkese*

Shoe Ah. Certain; i.e., "Victory is a shoe ah thing."
                                                          Bostonese

Shoplifter. A shopper with the gift of grab.
— A person who takes things for gratis.   *Harry Kabakoff*

SHOR, TOOTS. A bloated midget. *Bert Lahr*
— A world authority on lentil soup. *Gene Fowler*

SHORE, VIOLA BROTHERS. The seacoast of Bohemia.

SHORT VACATION. Half a loaf. *Vesta M. Kelly*

SHOTGUN. A weapon used to bring down bridegrooms and other birds.
— An officer under the Mikado. *Anon., Jr.*

SHOULDER STRAP. What keeps an attraction from becoming a sensation. *Anon. collegiate*

SHOUTING. Raising the level of the voice instead of the intelligence.

SHOVER. A professional driver, as: "Besides being Lady Chatterley's gamekeeper, he was her shover." *New Yorkese*

SHOWMAN. A politician who risks election every day.

SHROUD. A bad habit.

SHYSTER. The other fellow's lawyer. *C. Henry Gordon*
(SIC). An editorial sneer at a grammatical errer (sic).
— The device by which the editor sics the reader onto the writer.

SILENCE. The mother of truth. *Disraeli*
— The most perfect expression of scorn.
George Bernard Shaw
— The art of conversation. *William Hazlitt*
— The unbearable repartee. *G. K. Chesterton*
— Having nothing to say, and saying it.
— The highest wisdom of a fool. *Francis Quarles*
— A conversation with an Englishman. *Heinrich Heine*
— What you don't hear when you listen.
— Often guilt instead of golden. *Hal Cochran*
— Silence is not always golden. Sometimes it's just plain yellow. *Anon.*

SIMILE. A widening of the face when pleased. *Anon., Jr.*
— A picturesque way of saying what you really mean, such as calling your mother an old trout. *Ibid.* (*British Division*)

SIMPLETON. A local yokel.

SIN. Stealing apples. *Leonard Neubauer**

SINATRA, FRANK. The stiff that dreams are made of.

SINCERE. Without wax. *Original meaning*
SINCERE FRIEND. One who says nasty things to your face, instead of saying them behind your back. *Anon., Jr.*

SINECURE. The surest cure for a cynic. *Maurice Hanline**

SINGER, BLUES. Someone who makes every day sound like Yom Kippur. *Lionel Hampton*

SINGULAR. What a man is if he isn't married by the time he is thirty-five. *Margaret McKeever Ellert*

SINISTER. One who sins. *College Humor*
— A woman who hasn't married. *Anon., Jr.*

SINKING FUND. A place where they hide the profits from the stockholders. Boston *Transcript*

SINNER. A man who makes no pretensions to being good on one day out of seven. *Mary Wilson Little*

SINN FEIN. An Irish club.

SIREN. A scream or a dream.
— What a woman looks like before marriage and sounds like after. *Arthur Murray*
— A dangerous woman often found in factories. *Anon., Jr.*
SIRENS. Ladies in the middle of the ocean. Nobody could come near them, they made so much noise. *Anon., Jr.*

SIRLOIN. The only article of clothing worn by Gandhi, the leader of India. *Anon., Jr.*

SISAL PLANT. A daffodil weighing 300 pounds.
Eldred F. Hitchcock

Skeleton. A stripteaser who overdid it. *Anon.*
— A man with his inside out and his outside off. *Anon., Jr.*

Skepticism. The ability to disbelieve anything.

Skier. One who jumps to contusions. *Nancy Whear*
    skiing. Whoosh! Then walk a mile. *Anon. Indian*

Skull. The house you live in.

Skullduggery. Robbing a grave to bemoan Yorick.

Skunk. A community scenter. *Anon.*

Skylark. The leading character in *The Merchant of Venice*.
Anon., Jr.

Skyscraper. A building with its own barber shop.

Slander. The poisoned breath of scandal.

Slang. Language serving its apprenticeship.
Henry Thomas Buckle, 1860
— Sport-model language stripped down to get more speed
    with less horsepower. Buffalo *Evening News*
— The bright lexicon of youth.
— Zingo-Lingo.

Slave. Anyone compelled to work for his food, lodging, and
    clothing.
    slavery. The enlistment of labor on a sustenance basis;
        now forbidden except in the restricted form of marriage.
    — A condition from which some of the colored races have
        been freed.

Sleep. An excellent way of listening to an opera.
James Stephens
— A cure for yawning.
— A holiday from reality. *Victor Ratner*
— Death's younger brother. *Mary Anthers*
— Still the best eraser in the world. *O. A. Battista*
    sleeping bag. A napsack. *Anon. collegiate*

SLIDE RULE. An instrument for extending guesswork to the third place.

SLOGAN. A war cry in business.

SLOT MACHINE. Something that makes money by not working.
                                    Cynic's Cyclopaedia
— The only thing that can stand with its back to the wall and defy the world.   *Goodman Ace*

SLUM. A place with the earmark of an eyesore.
                                    *Paul Oehser**

SMALL TOWN. Where everybody knows what everybody else is doing—and all buy the weekly newspaper to see how much the editor dares to print. *New Hampshire newsman*
— A place where a fellow has to walk around a dog enjoying a nap on the sidewalk.   *A. W. Perrine*
— A place where there is nothing to buy with money.
                                    Rebecca West
— A place where everybody knows whose check is good and whose wife isn't. *Jack Sterling's Anti-collegiate Dictionary*

SMILE. The whisper of a laugh.   *Anon., Jr.*
— A slip of the pan.   *Leonard Neubauer**

SMOCK. A shirt on the loose.

GENERAL SMUTS. What all the different black races are called in the northwestern quarter of Africa.
                        Anon., Jr. (*British Division*)
SNACKS. Weight lifters.

SNAKE EYES. The point of no return.

SNEER. An unspeakable insult.

SNERD, MORTIMER. A fugitive from a butter churn.
                                    Charlie McCarthy
SNICKER. A leaky chuckle.

SNIGGER. To snicker up one's nose.

SNOB. One who worships mean things meanly.
W. M. Thackeray
— A lady who walks like a peacock.   *Patience Abbe*
— One who holds her head so high she has a double chin on
the back of her neck.   *Molly McGee*
— One who suffers from claustrophobia of the heart.
Cyril Connolly
— A cobbler's helper—in other words, a person of lowly posi-
tion.   *Early meaning*

SNOOD. A net to catch hairs.
— A bustle a woman wears on her brains.   *Don Quinn**

SNORE. To sleep out loud.
  SNORING. Letting off sleep.   *Anon., Jr. (British Division)*
  — The tuneful serenade of that wakeful nightingale, the
  nose.   *George Farquhar*

SNUFF-MAKER. A man who goes around sticking his business
in other people's noses.   *Don Quinn**

SOBRIETY. Training yourself for a respectable set of pall-
bearers.

SOCIAL. Afraid to go to bed alone.
  SOCIAL CLIMBER. A hodcarrier on the ladder of society.
  SOCIAL LEADER. A flake off the upper crust.
  SOCIALITE. A clubwoman whose husband advertises.

SOCIALISM. The survival of the unfit.   *Elbert Hubbard*
— The retreat from Moscow.
— A system which is workable only in heaven, where it isn't
needed, and in hell, where they've got it.
Cecil Palmer
  SOCIALIST. A man suffering from an overwhelming com-
  pulsion to believe what is not true.   *H. L. Mencken*
  — A man who goes to parties all the time.   *Anon., Jr.*

SOCIETY. Mankind, between quitting and sleeping.
— A hospital of incurables.   *Ralph Waldo Emerson*
  SOCIETY COLUMNIST. A man with a white tie and long tales.
Oscar Bradley

SOFA. A convertible without wheels.

SOKOLSKY, GEORGE E. A capitalist agitator.

SOLDIER. The only carnivorous animal that lives in a gregarious state.   *Johann Georg Zimmerman*
— A man hired to murder in a good cause.
— A guy who gets a piece of gold on his chest for a piece of lead in his pants.   *Jay C. Flippen*
SOLDIER OF FORTUNE. A gorilla in uniform.

SOLEMNITY. A trick of the body to hide the faults of the mind.   *La Rochefoucauld*

SOLOMON. A king with 300 wives and 700 porcupines.
          Anon., Jr.

SOLVENT. When you don't bother to smooth down your hair before entering your bank.

SOMNAMBULIST. One who wakes up in a strange bedroom.
— A man who writes a novel.   *Anon., Jr. (British Division)*

SONG. Poetry with sound effects.
   SONG PLUGGER. A musical Mickey Finn.   *Bob Hope*
   SONG WRITER. A pickpocket with a poetic license.

SOPHISTICATION. The art of getting drunk with the right people.

SOPRANO (Wagnerian). A blimp fitted with a calliope.
          H. L. Mencken

SORDID. Lifelike.

SORROW. The future tense of love.

SOTS. Different groups, as: "It takes all sots to make a whirl."
          New Yorkese

SOTTO VOCE. In a drunken voice.   *Anon., Jr.*

SOUGHT. A seasoning. Frequently "sought and paper."
          New Yorkese

SOUND STAGE. (Hollywood) A large padded cell.

SOUP. What people eat at the top of their voices.
Henry F. Gruhler

SOUTHERN GENTLEMAN. A guy who hasn't made love to his wife for five years and will shoot any other guy who tries to. *Anon.*

SOVIET. A cloth used by waiters in hotels. *Anon., Jr.*
SOVIET FOREIGN POLICY. An iron hand combined with a boardinghouse reach. Portland *Oregonian*

SPA. A place where people drink bath water. *Cecil Hunt, Jr.*

SPANIARD. A Catholic Moor. *John Gunther*

SPANISH MAIN. A boat which played an important part in history. It was sunk in the harbor of Havana. *Anon., Jr.*

SPANK. To impress upon the mind from the bottom up.
SPANKING. Punishment that takes less time than reasoning and penetrates sooner to the seat of memory.
Will Durant
— Manual training.
— Applause backwards.

SPECIALIST. A man who knows more and more about less and less. *Dr. William J. Mayo*

SPECTER. A man who doesn't believe in things like Santa Claus. *Anon., Jr.*

SPECTRUM. The rainbow division.

SPEECH. An effort by a speaker to make an assemblage return the compliment of his presence by the acceptance of his ideas.
— Pulling the haystack apart to disclose the needle.
MAJOR SPEECH. An address in which a candidate calls his opponent a big bum instead of a little one.
Boston Journal

SPEECHLESS. The condition of a speaker who only wants to say a few words—over and over for a few hours.

SPEED. To expectorate: "The lore says 'Don't speed on the sidewalk.'" *New Yorkese*

SPEEDER. An ambulance chaser. *Leonard Neubauer**

SPICE. The plural of spouse. *Anon., Jr. (British Division)*

SPINE. A long, limber bone. Your head sets on one end and you set on the other. *Anon., Jr.*
— A dead-end street. *Don Quinn**
    SPINAL COLUMN. A collection of bones running up and down your back which keeps you from being legs clean up to your neck. *Anon., Jr.*

SPINSTER. A woman who has been Missed too long.
— A vintage virgin.
— A bachelor's wife. *Anon., Jr.*
— A woman who knows all the answers but has never been asked the question.
    Earlene White, President National Association of Business & Professional Women

SPIT. To drive at an excessive rate. "It is also against the lore to take your caw and spit on the sidewalk." *New Yorkese*
— (cookery) A poke in a pig.

SPITE. Anger which is afraid to show itself. *Amiel's Journal*

SPIVS. People who work in ways the government hasn't thought of. *Anon., Jr. (British Division)*

SPLIT SECOND. The interval between the time when the light turns green and the man behind starts blowing his horn.
    Aztec

SPLURGE. A wet surge. *Anon.*
    SURGE. A dry splurge.

SPOILS OF WAR. Army food. *Anon.*

SPOON. A small shovel for the mouth.

SPORTS EXPERT. The guy who writes the best alibis for being wrong. *Jimmy Cannon, sports expert*

SPORTSMAN. One who gets tired standing all day over a hot golf course. *Don Quinn**

SPOUSE. The opposite of spice. *Eugene Archer*

SPRING. Nature taking up its option on the world.
   SPRING MEETING. A series of horse races held in snowstorms. *Jimmy Cannon*

SPUDS. Athletic activities. *New Yorkese*

SQUARE. A somewhat opaque, insensitive and unresponsive fellow, unaware of the nuances of contemporary thought; it has something to do with his sense of humor, but that isn't it exactly. *Cmdr. Edward Whitehead*
— The other fellow. *Rod Reed*

STABLE. A horse house.

STACK. Sheer, utter. Especially, "stack naked." *Bostonese*

STAGGER. The shortest distance between two pints.

STALIN. The soul of an Oriental despot. *Lenin*
— The most outstanding mediocrity of Soviet bureaucracy.
   Trotsky
— The Russian Father Divine. *Sinclair Lewis*

STAR. Somebody's sun.
— A comet with a short tale. *Morton Thompson*
   STARLET. A girl who's pushed her shelf to the front.
     — A girl a studio pays to learn to act while she's looking for a husband. *Tom Jenk*

STATESMAN. A diplomat with a diploma.
— A Congressman seeking re-election.   *Leonard Neubauer**
— A politician away from home.   *Anon.*
— A dead politician.   *Thomas B. Reed*
  ELDER STATESMAN. A politically dead politician.
    Harry S Truman
  STATESMANSHIP. The wise employment of individual mean-
    nesses for the public good.   *Abraham Lincoln*

STATISTICS. Mendacious truths.   *Lionel Strachey*
  STATISTICIAN. A man who draws a mathematically precise
    line from an unwarranted assumption to a foregone con-
    clusion.   *Anon.*
— A liar who can figure.

STATUS QUO. Latin for "de mess we's in."   *Uncle Tom*

STEAM. Water gone crazy with the heat.   *Mickey Mouse*

STEEL WOOL. The shearing from a hydraulic ram.   *Anon., Jr.*

STEER. A bull that has lost his social standing.
    Dude's Dictionary

STENOGRAPHER. A girl you pay to learn how to spell while
  she's looking for a husband.   *Franklin P. Jones*

-STER. A female suffix, as will be seen in spinster, monster
  and sterile.   *Anon., Jr. (British Division)*

STEVENSON, ROBERT LOUIS. An author who got married and
  went on his honeymoon. It was then he wrote *Travels with
  a Donkey*.   *Anon., Jr.*

STOICISM. The quality that keeps a woman smiling when a
  departing guest stands at the open screen door and lets the
  flies in.   *Anon.*

STOLID. A young fillum address.   *New Yorkese*

STOMACH. The home of the swallow.
    Anon., Jr. (British Division)

— The organ of indigestion. *Anon., Jr.*
— Something to hold up petticoats. *Ibid., Jr.*

Stooge. A guy who lives by the wrong side of the cracks.
Rod Maclean

Stool Pigeon. A fowl of the law.

Stowe, Harriet Beecher. Uncle Tom's mother.

Straight. Without ginger ale. *Anon. collegiate*

Strait Jacket. A garment used to prevent madmen from biting their nails.

Strategy. To keep firing when you are out of ammunition.
Anon., Jr.

Straw Hat. A Wheatie wig.

Straw Vote. An indication of which way the hot air blows.
O. Henry

Street. A broad flat surface used for the storage of No Parking signs. *Wall Street Journal*

Strike. A labor pain.

Striptease. Exposure with composure.
strip teaser. A girl who looks well in anything she takes off. *Gypsy Rose Lee**

Strut. The walk o' the cock.

Studio. A smokehouse where hams are cured in the golden smoke of burning dividends. *Morton Thompson**

Stuffed Pepper. A hamburger with a girdle. *Milton Berle*

Style. The official selection of the parts of women's bodies that will be looked at this season.

Submarine. A battleship that dunks. *Anon.*

Subscription. Something that works a young man's way through college for him when he can't play football.

SUBLIME. Heaven à la king.

SUBTLE. Weeping in the shower.
    SUBTLETY. The art of saying what you want to say and getting out of range before it is understood.
The Wyatt Way

SUBURBS. A kind of healthy grave.   *Sydney Smith*

SUBVERSION. A political science made up of sedition, detraction, mystification, and subdivision.

SUBWAY. A thundering bore.

SUCCESS. The mechanical rabbit in the dog-eat-dog race.
— A chemical compound of man with moment.
Philip Guedalla
— Making more money so you can pay off the taxes you wouldn't have to pay if you didn't have so much money already.   *Anon.*
— A matter either of getting around you better men than yourself or getting around better men than yourself.
Banking
— Getting what you want.
    HAPPINESS. Wanting what you get.   *Anon.*
    LUCK. An explanation of the other fellows' success.
Harry Thompson
    ABILITY. The explanation of your success.   *Ibid.*

SUCKER LIST. A lollypop ledger.   *Horatio K. Boomer*

SUICIDE. The severest form of self-criticism.

SUMMER. The season of inferior sledding. *Eskimo definition*
— The part of the year an Indian doesn't have to wear underwear.   *Shorty Tall Horse*
    INDIAN SUMMER. The six weeks you spend every fall putting off having the furnace fixed.   *Mrs. Wally Boren*

SUN. A small star, one of whose smaller satellites is inhabited.
    SETTING SUN. The red taillight of the departing day.
Richard Kinney

SUNDAY. The day of arrest. *Wellman L. France*
  SUNDAY DRIVER. A guy who left the house on Friday. *Anon.*
  SUNDAY SCHOOL. A prison in which children do penance
    for the evil conscience of their parents. *H. L. Mencken*
  — An institution that tells children about God for fifty-one
    weeks and then introduces them to Santa Claus.

SUNDAY, BILLY. Savonarola with a blackjack. *Gene Fowler*

SUNNY. The foist day of the wick. *New Yorkese*

SUNSET. The day's westfallen ember. *Christopher Morley*

SUNSTROKE. The heat you wanted last winter.

SUPERHIGHWAY. A road system which succeeds in giving us
  wider traffic jams. *Monty Babson*

SUPERIORITY. The feeling you get when riding on an express
  train and pass a local. *Glenn C. Fowler*

SUPERSTITION. Belief in a bureaucracy of vindictive spirits
  beyond the control of civil service.

SUPERVISOR. (Hollywood) A studio executive who asks you
  a question, gives you the answer, and then tells you you're
  wrong. *Harry Hirshfield**
  — The kind of a guy you'd use for a blueprint if you were
    building an idiot. *Hugh Herbert*

SUPREME COURT. A group of men who don't care who make
  the nation's laws.
  — The A.K.'s who give the O.K.'s.
    George S. Kaufman & Morrie Ryskind

SURFEIT. An apron worn in the front. *Anon., Jr.*

SURREALISM. Arrested development. *Don Herold*

SUSPENSE. The life of a spider. *Jonathan Swift*

SUSPICION. The friendship that one actress has for another.
  Eleonora Duse

SWANKY. That's where the dames wear hats and the guys don't.   *Anon.*

DEAN SWIFT. An inveterate if sloppy punster.
                                                    Clifton Fadiman

SWIMMER. A pool shark.
  SWIMMING HOLE. A body of water completely surrounded by boys.   *Suburban Life*
  SWIMMING POOL. A crowd of people with water in it.
                                                    Hutchinson Habit

SWINDLER. A character who is quick on the trickery.

SWING MUSIC. Din and jitters.   *Horace Heidt*
— Where the drums carry the melody.   *George Meyer*

SWITZERLAND. A very wonderful place, you can often see the mountains touring among the clouds.
                                Anon., Jr. (British Division)
— A country of perilous prospects and cautious views.
— Beautiful but dumb.   *Edna Ferber*

SYMPATHIZER. A fellow that's for you as long as it doesn't cost anything.   *Kin Hubbard*
  SYMPATHY. Subconscious self-pity.   *Harry Ruby*
— Two hearts tugging at the same load.
                                                Charles Parkhurst
— What one girl offers another in exchange for details.
                                                        Judge

SYNONYM. A word you use when you cannot spell the other.
                                                        Grit

SYNTAX. All the money collected by the church from sinners.
                                                    Anon., Jr.

SYZYGY. Something which, when seen, can't be pronounced either.   *Bob Murphy*

T

T. The model for the first crucifix. It was common along the roads of Rome following the defeat of Spartacus, who had the mistaken notion that slaves were the equals of masters. It is also the first letter in *trouble,* a word which is perhaps too obvious to be included in this dictionary. However, the word *trousers* is included, which evidently means the same thing . . . to the editors. It also leads off *truth,* many superficial definitions of which are given in this book. Pilate, washing his hands of it and blandly asking what it was, came nearer to it than all the makers of definitions. The poor fellow, over whom he was troubled concerning truth, died on a crucifix between two other men in search of it, in the red dusk of a day that will never end so long as men will not learn to laugh at themselves, in the words of Nietzsche, who laughed at himself and died mad.

The letter T was used by the one time stationary engineer for his most popular model. That many men toil a lifetime and are never able to have enough money to completely pay for one of the damn things is the reason it is called a Model T. T stands for truth—as evanescent as money with a factory worker.

T bows in *Tullius,* last name of Cicero. He thought he heard Truth walking down the aisle of a Roman Pullman. He stuck his head between the curtains and another searcher cut it off. Thus died the apostle of Truth, brilliant, forceful, cowardly, opportunistic, as are all its disciples who followed after him.

T is also Tully—who met Truth, and found her a whore with an imaginary maidenhead. She was abject, fawning, sinuous, lecherous, charming as May weather and gay with all delight. She then became the drab of passion, with skirts that did not fit and hair in disarray—a withered bag of bones waiting for the horse of death. *Jim Tully°*

TABLOID. A newspaper for those who move their lips when they look at pictures.

TACT. The ability to describe others as they see themselves.
Abraham Lincoln
— The knack of making a point without making an enemy.
Howard W. Newton
— Letting someone have your own way. *Ben Roberts°*
— Making guests feel at home when you wish they were.
Anon.
— The unsaid part of what you think. *Henry Van Dyke*
TACTLESSNESS. The unthought part of what you say.

TAHITI. The bughouse of the Pacific. *Donald Barr Chidsey*

TAIL. An organ of emotion that man has outgrown.

TAILOR. A sew-and-sew. *Don Quinn°*

TALK. The greatest of all Jewish sports. *Harry Golden*
TALKING. Painting to the ear. *Joseph Joubert*
— The occupational disease of women.
— The disease of age. *Ben Jonson*
— The theory that you can get somewhere if you keep putting one word in front of the other.

TANTRUM. A two-seated bicycle. *Anon., Jr.*

TAPIOCA. Proletarian caviar. *Frank Loesser°*
— The Zasu Pitts of desserts. *Dorothy Gulman°*

TART. A cutie pie.

TARZAN. Cinderella, with muscles.
— A short name for the American flag. Its full name is Tarzan Stripes. *Anon., Jr. (British Division)*

TASTE. A leaning toward the styles you admire. *Anon.*

TATTOO. Personal art.   *Ruth K. Levinson**
— Skin scenery.

TAVERN. A place where madness is sold by the bottle.
Jonathan Swift

TAX. The outgo of the income.   *Bob Levinson**
TAXES. The dues charged to belong to a country.
— The price of civilization. *Justice Oliver Wendell Holmes*
— The other certainty.
TAXPAYER. A fellow who has exchanged his place in the
sun for one behind the eight ball.
— One who doesn't have to pass a civil service exam to
work for the government.

TEA. A stimulant, a thirst quencher, and a drug, the greatest
English common denominator.   *Tony Mayer*
— A widow's weed.
— An affront to luncheon and an insult to dinner.
Mark Twain
PINK TEA. Giggle—gabble—gobble—git.
Oliver Wendell Holmes

TEACHING. The liquidation of illiteracy.   *British Officialese*

TEAM. A mutual protection society formed to guarantee that
no one person can be held to blame for a botched committee job that one man could have performed satisfactorily.
Russell Baker

TEARS. A good-bye product.
— The juice of the emotions.
— The world's greatest waterpower. *En-ar-co National News*

TECHNIQUE. In essence the ability to get the biggest possible
effect with the least possible effort.   *Richard Burton*

TECHNOCRACY. Communism with spats.   *John C. Stevens*
— Socialism by slide rule.

TEETH. Grind organs.

TEETOTALER. A man who you never see drinking. *Anon., Jr.*

TELEPHONE. A device by which personal conversation can be interrupted from great distances.

    TELEPHONE BOOTH. A vertical coffin where sweet dispositions are buried. *Ed Wynn*

TELEVISION. A device that enables you to see static as well as hear it. *Anon. collegiate*
— A dim view of life.
— Chewing gum for the eyes. *Frank Lloyd Wright*
— Smog with knobs. *Bob Hope*
— The triumph of machinery over people. *Fred Allen*
— The longest amateur night in history. *Robert Carson*
— Radio fluoroscoped. *Fred Allen*
— Where all little movies go when they're bad. *Ron Poulton*
— A kind of radio which lets people at home see what the studio audience is not laughing at. *Fred Allen*
— Like seeing someone you know at the bottom of a dish of jello. *Bob Hope*
— A device that permits people who haven't anything to do to watch people who can't do anything. *Fred Allen*
— A remarkable medium. You have to work five or six years in the theater, in hit shows, to make people sick and tired of you. This you can accomplish in only a few weeks of television. *Walter Slezak*

    TELEVISION COMMERCIAL. The last refuge of optimism in a world of gloom. *Sir Cedric Hardwicke*
    — The opening and closing quarter hours of a half-hour show. *Bona Venture*

    TELEVISION CRITICISM. Like trying to explain an accident.
        Jackie Gleason

WILLIAM TELL. A man who shot an arrow through an apple while standing on his son's head. *Anon., Jr.*

TEMPER. The banana skin of intelligence.
    TEMPERAMENT. A pretty woman's nasty temper.
    — Temper that is too old to spank. *Charlotte Greenwood*

TEMPERATE ZONE. The region where no one drinks too much.
Anon., Jr. (British Division)

TENNYSON. A poet who betrayed women very successfully.
Anon., Jr.

TENTERHOOKS. The upholstery of the anxious seat.
Robert E. Sherwood

TERM-AIDER. A red wedge-able.   *New Yorkese*

TERN-AIDER. A gnawful big wind.   *Ibid.*

TERRAPIN. An angel of the highest order.   *Anon., Jr.*

TERROR. A canine, as: "They got a duck, a fogs terror."
New Yorkese

TERSE DAY. The fit day of the wick.   *New Yorkese*

TESTATOR. A rich man who leaves nothing to chance.

TEXAS. A place with more cows and less milk, more rivers
and less water, and you can look farther and see less than
anywhere else on earth. (You even have to climb for water
and dig for wood.)   *Visiting senator*

THAMES. Liquid history.   *John Burns*
— At once London's highroad and its sewer.
John Harold Wilson

THANKS. A down payment on the next favor.

THEATRE. A method of obtaining money by false pretenses.

THEOLOGY. A tool to make angels out of fools.

THEOREM. Derived from "theos," a god, and "res," a thing—
is a problem needing Divine intelligence.
Anon., Jr. (British Division)

THEORY. A hunch with a college education.   *J. A. Carter*

THERMOMETER. An instrument for raising temperance.
Anon., Jr.

THIEF. One who just has a habit of finding things before people lose them.   *Joe E. Lewis*

THINKING. What a great many people think they are doing when they are merely rearranging their prejudices.
                                                            William James

"THIS IS YOUR LIFE". A program specially designed to transform one man's embarrassment into sentimental entertainment for the millions.   *London TV critic*

THOUGHT. A son of a wish. (The wish is father to the thought.)

THOUSAND ISLAND DRESSING. Mayonnaise with bumps.

THRIFT. A wonderful virtue—especially in ancestors.
                                            Fort Wadsworth *Range-Finder*

THROMBOSIS. An instrument used in a jazz band and something like a slip horn.   *Anon., Jr.*

THUNDER. A weather report.

TICK. The death knell of a second.

TICKET. Closely planted bushes. A junior fur rest.
                                                            New Yorkese

TIGHTWAD. One who pinches those little creases at the edge of coins.   *Fibber McGee*

TIMBER. Wood between tree and lumber.

TIME. The most popular murder victim.
— The stuff between paydays.   *Scott Field Broadcaster*
— A great healer but a very poor beauty doctor.
                                                    Anon. collegiate
— A flowing river.   *Christopher Morley*
    TIME MAGAZINE. A periodical with all the faults of a newspaper and none of its virtues.   *Silas Bent*
    — Misinformation trimmed with insult.   *Jacques Barzun*

TIN SIN STOW. The foive and doyme. *Charlestonese*

TIP. A sum of money that is more than you can afford and less than the waiter expected. *Cynic's Cyclopaedia*
TIPS. Wages we pay other people's help. *Anon.*

TIP-EGG. A thing you soak in hut warder to get a cop dee. *New Yorkese*

TOASTMASTER. A guy who goes around introducing guys who need no introduction. *Stetson U. Reporter*
— The punk that sets off the fireworks. *Gene Buck*
— A man who eats a meal he doesn't want so he can get up and tell a lot of stories he doesn't remember to a lot of people who've already heard them. *George Jessel*

TODAY. Yesterday's effect and tomorrow's cause. *Philip Gribble*

TOBACCO. The only excuse for Columbus's misadventure in discovering America. *Sigmund Freud*

TOLERANCE. Slamming the window instead of the next-door neighbor.

TOMATO. A soft answer.

TOMBSTONE. A precaution taken by rich young widows.

TOMORROW. One of the greatest labor-saving inventions of today. *Vincent T. Foss*
— The day you go on the diet. *Anon.*
— Always the busiest day of the week. *Richard Willis*

TOM TOM. The piper's son.

TONE. Ripped. *Charlestonese*

TONGUE. The neck's enemy. *Arabian proverb*
— A concealed weapon.

TONSORIALIST. A barber who splits hairs.

TONSURE. A priest's shaving his head instead of cutting it off.
Anon., Jr.

TOOLS. Artificial hands.
CHISEL. A stronger fingernail.
HAMMER. A harder fist.
KNIFE. A long wedge.
SAW. A set of artificial teeth.

TORCH. A brand snatched from the burning to become a banner.

TOREADOR. The power behind the thrown.   *Elbert Hubbard*

TORN. A vegetable needle, as: "She's a torn in my sight."
New Yorkese

TORTOISE. An animal that let its hare down.

TORTURE. Sitting in a barber's chair with your mouth full of lather, watching the boy trying to give another customer your new hat.   Dartmouth *Jack o' Lantern*

TORY. A politician who is definitely one-sided.
Anon., Jr. (British Division)

TOTEM POLE. An Indian's family tree.   *R. L. Ripley*
— Father Divine with splinters.

TOUPEE. A top secret.

TOUCHDOWN. The clown in *As You Like It.*   *Anon., Jr.*

TOURIST. A guy who travels 5,000 miles to have his picture taken in front of his car.   *Anon.*

TOUT. A guy who never had anything, never will have anything, but to you he gives everything.   *Jack Kenny*

TOWER OF BABEL. A place where Solomon kept his wives.
Anon., Jr.

TOWN. A congested spot between two parking spaces.
College Humor

TOXICOLOGIST. A guy who can really name your poison.

TOYS. Life in miniature.
                    Philip Kirkham, former toy-store president

TRADE MARK. The branding iron of business.

TRADE UNION. A place to which a workman goes when he
    gets the sack.   *Anon., Jr. (British Division)*

TRADITION. An unwritten law that nobody dares to bust on
    account of if they do, it'll be made into a written law
    and somebody's liable to repeal it, and then the fat's in
    the fire. You can't repeal a tradition.   *Fibber McGee*

TRAFFIC SIGNAL. A green light that changes to red as your
    car approaches.

TRAGEDY. Comedy turned upside down.
— Living alone and liking it.   *Dorothy Gulman**
— In this world there are only two—one is not getting what
    one wants, and the other is getting it.   *Oscar Wilde*

TRAILER (movie). A warning to next week's patrons.
                                        Groucho Marx
— (auto). A house looking for a lot.

TRAITOR. A bad subject.
— A California doctor who advises a change of climate for a
    patient.   *Wilcox Antenna*

TRANSLATOR. One who does not know what a foreign author
    means, but is willing to explain.
    TRANSLATING. Siphoning a bottle of wine into a pail of
        water.

TRANSPARENT. Something you can see through, such as a key-
    hole.   *Anon., Jr.*
— A cross father.   *Anon., Jr. (British Division)*

TRAVEL. A fool's paradise.   *Ralph Waldo Emerson*
    TRAVELING. Either an experience we shall always remem-
        ber, or one we shall never forget.   *Rabbi Julius Gordon*
    TRAVEL FOLDER. A trip tease.   *Anon.*

TRAVESTY. Imitation without flattery.

TREATY. An agreement between nations who cross their hearts and cross their fingers. *Leonard Neubauer**

TREE. The only umbrella you can't borrow.
— A thing that will stand in one place fifty years and then suddenly jump in front of a woman driver.
Banana River Peelings

TRENTON. To utter threads, i.e., "Snow use trying to trenton me." *New Yorkese*

TRESPASS. To step on another's corn.

TRIAL HORSE. A heavyweight picking up money so he can afford to live in a private sanitarium when he quits fighting.
Jimmy Cannon.

TRIANGLE. A circle with three corners to it. *Anon., Jr.*

TRIFLER. A hit-and-run lover. *Oliver Herford*

TRIGONOMETRY. When a lady marries three men at the same time. *Anon., Jr.*

TRILEMMA. A three-sided dilemma. *John Gunther*

TROJAN HORSE. A phony pony.

TROLLOPE, ANTHONY. A word-factory. (He produced words wholesale and sold them at retail.) *Anthony Trollope*

TROUBLE. Somethin' I cain't fix. *Oklahoma farmer*
— A baby that grows larger with nursing. *Lady Holland*
— The one product in which the supply exceeds the demand.
Anon.

TROUSERS. An uncommon noun because it is singular on top and plural at the bottom. *Anon., Jr.*

TROUSSEAU. What a bride wears for five years after the wedding. *Mindy Carson*

TRUANCY. Something which has been proven to be true.
Anon., Jr.

TRUANT OFFICER. A talent scout for a reform school.
Charlie McCarthy

TRUE. Hurled, i.e., "He true the ball." *New Yorkese*
TRUE LOVE. Marrying the girl even though she doesn't
have a steady job. *G. Norman Collie*

TRUTH. A suspicion that has endured. *Ramón de Campoamor*
— A hallucination agreed upon by a majority.
— Courage. *Hosea Ballou*
— The first casualty in time of war. *Boake Carter*
— A good dog; but beware of barking too close to the heels
of an error, lest you get your brains kicked out.
Samuel Taylor Coleridge
— Not a diet but a condiment. *Christopher Morley*
— An error in the right direction.

TUNE. A pattern of sounds.

TURNPIKE. The long lane that has no turning. *Clyde Moore*

TWAIN, MARK. The Lincoln of literature.
William Dean Howells

TWILIGHT. The difference between day and night.

TWIN. A double take.
TWINS. Wombmates. *Culler MacRaw*

TWIST. A dance which shakes everything below the ears.

TYPEWRITER. A boon to authors, as it enables them to say
more and mean less than any other invention. *Will Cuppy*

TZIMMES. A one-dish meal usually served as the fourth course
of a six-course dinner. *Sara Kasdan*

U

UGANDA. . . . This glittering equatorial slum . . .
                                        Sir Winston Churchill

UGLY. Having just left the beauty parlor.

UKULELE. The missing link between music and noise.
                                        Prof. E. K. Kruger

ULCER. A wound stripe of civilization.   *Fortune*

ULTIMATUM. The last fifty thousand words.

ULYSSES. A man whose adventures should have been a warning to wandering husbands.

UMBRELLA. A portable roof.
— Civilization defying the elements.

UMPIRE. A judge of diamonds.

UNBEARABLE. Acting like a bear.

UNBEND. To straighten a bend or to bend from the straight.
   UNBENT. Made straight or (as the case may be) unstraight.

UNBIASED. Having the same bias you have. *The Colonel Says*

UNBRIDLED ORGY. A wild horse.   *Anon., Jr.*

UNCLE TOM'S CABIN. A station on the underground railway.
                                        Anon., Jr.

UNCORRUPTED. Untempted.

UNDERSTANDING. Mutual praise and pity.   *Dorothy Parker*

UNDERSTATEMENT. A British trick of saying less in order to convey more.   *Tony Mayer*

UNDERSTUDY. A substitute to remind a star that the show can go on without him.

UNDERTAKER. The boxer who always wins.
— The guy who in the end always lets you down.
UNDERTAKING PARLOR. The beauty shop of the dead.

UNEDUCATED. Getting by on your raw brains.

UNEMPLOYMENT. A breakdown of the economic system in which there is no money to pay workers because the workers have no money to buy goods, because there is no money to pay workers, because they have no money to buy goods, etc., etc.
— A cure for peace.

UNFAITHFUL. Having nothing to say to your husband because you've already said everything to someone else.
Françoise Sagan

UNHAPPINESS. Not knowing what we want and killing ourselves to get it. *Don Herold*

UNIFORM. Sheep's clothing.

UNION SUIT. Under-overalls.
— A portal-to-portal undergarment.

UNIVERSITY. An institution of physical training where certain intellectual discipline is especially provided for feeble-bodied students. *Anon. Chinese student*
— A college with a stadium seating over 40,000.
— An institution of higher yearning.
Princeton Seminary Bulletin
— An institution of higher yawning.
— An institution for the postponement of experience.

UNMARRIED. Not caught.

UNPOPULAR. Having just won a popularity contest.

UNRELENTING. Ordering that your ashes be thrown into your enemy's face.

UNSPEAKABLE. Beyond pronunciation or denunciation.

UNUTTERABLE. A thought for which the words haven't been invented yet.

UPPER BERTH. A room where you rise to retire and get down from when you get up.

UPPER CRUST. Nothing but a bunch of crumbs stuck together with their own dough.   *Fibber McGee*

URGE. To request with a push.

USURER. A man who takes too much interest in his business.
                                                        Anon.

UTAH. An Indian tribe now exiled to a reservation in Colorado.

UTOPIA. A place where democracy really works.
— Any place where there are no people.   *Harry Ruby*

V

VACATION. Time off, to remind employees that the business can get along without them.

— What you take when you can no longer take what you've been taking. *Earl Wilson*

VACATIONER. A person who thinks people back home care how many blankets he is sleeping under.

J. A. Crevierre

VACCINE. A microbe with his face washed. *Frank Scully*

VACUUM. An empty space where the Pope lives.

Anon., Jr. (British Division)

VACUUM CLEANER. A collective noun.*

Pennsylvania Punch Bowl

— A broom with a stomach. *Anon.*

VAGABOND. A sissy tramp. *John McDermott**

VAGRANT. A tough tramp.

VALEDICTORY. The climax of a college education.

— A demonstration of how to wave bye-bye with the tongue.

VALET. An English gintilman who has arose be conscientious wurruk to th' position iv a bootjack. *Mr. Dooley*

VALHALLA. The California of the dead. *Jim Tully**

VANDAL. A painter of mustaches.

VANISHING LINES. Those that get nearer together as they get further apart. *Anon., Jr. (British Division)*

VAUDEVILLE. Smorgasbord in the theatre.

VAUDEVILLE ACTOR. Part gypsy and part suitcase.

Fred Allen

---

* Only 65 per cent collective.—*Consumers Research.*

VEGETABLE. A plant that people have learned to eat.
   VEGETABLE CELL. A place very dark and gloomy where greengrocers who sell bad vegetables go.
                                 Anon., Jr. (British Division)

VEGETARIAN. A person who eats no animal life that can be seen without a microscope.

VEIL. A curtain to let the imagination improve on nature.

VELOCITY. The thing which one lets go of a bee with.
                                 London Opinion

VENTRILOQUISM. Grunting as a fine art.   *Edgar Bergen*
   VENTRILOQUIST. A man who talks to himself for a living.
                                 Quentin Reynolds
— One who talks straight from the tummy.

VENUS. The goddess of love in the broader sense.   *Anon., Jr.*
   VENUS DE MILO. The goddess of disarmament.
— The result of statuary rape.

VERB. A word that enables a sentence to get somewhere.
— A passive verb is when the subject is the sufferer, as in "I am loved."   *The Grade Teacher*
   ACTIVE VERB. One that shows action.   *Anon., Jr.*
   PASSIVE VERB. One that shows passion.   *Ibid., Jr.*

VERDICT. The opinion of twelve men on a subject they don't understand.   *Cynic's Cyclopaedia*

VERLAINE, PAUL. A French poet who frequently lived like a pig and wrote like an angel.
— The bard sinister.

VERMILION. Bloodshot orange.

VERSION. The kind of Queen that Queen Elizabeth I was.
                                 Charlestonese

VET. A man who learned to fight for his country and then to fight for himself.

VETERINARIAN. A doctor who can't ask his patient questions.
David Harum

VICAR. The masculine of vixen. *Anon., Jr.*

VICE. A sin that's become a habit.

VICTIM. The unquick.

VILLAGE. A town where the elevation is higher than the population.

VILLAIN. One who believes all ladies are women.
George Jean Nathan

VIOLA. An instrument played by a disappointed second violinist. *Deems Taylor*

VIRGIN. Unraped, unwrapped, unaxed.
VIRGIN FOREST. A forest in which the hand of man has never set foot. *Anon., Jr.*

VIRTUE. A constant struggle against the laws of nature.
De Finod
— An inexpensive vice.
— Won't-power.
— A jewel—if a woman has no others.
— A quality which has never been as respectable as money.
Mark Twain
FEMININE VIRTUE. Lack of temptation. *Brown Jug*
MASCULINE VIRTUE. Lack of opportunity. *Ibid.*

VIRTUOSO. An artist that can draw a crowd.

VIRUS. A Latin medical term, meaning, "Your guess is as good as mine." *Anon.*
— Something a doctor says you have when he doesn't know what it is. *Al Bernie*
ALLERGY. Something a doctor says you have when he does know what it is—but doesn't know how to get rid of it.
Ibid.

Vision. What people think you have when you guess right.

Visit. An endurance test of companionship.

Vista. An opening in the landscape through which one can see a billboard.   *College Humor*

Vote. To choose the lesser of evils.

Vulgarity. A characteristic conspicuous among the civilized.

W

WAFFLE. A pancake with a nonskid tread.   *American Boy*

WAG. Either a dog's gaiety or a gay dog.

WAGNER. A melodramatic rhetorician of the senses.
Nietzsche

WAINSCOT. A waistcoat for a room.

WAISTCOAT. A vest purchased on purpose.

WAITER. A guy who believes that money grows on trays.
Walter Winchell
— The guy you have to see to get indigestion.   *Anon.*
   WAITRESS. A croquette croupier.   *Fibber McGee*

WAKE. The area of disturbance where a vessel has passed.
Don Quinn*
— A keen party.

WALL. A fool's paper.   *English proverb*
   WAILING WALL. A street in New York.
Northwestern Purple Parrot
   WALLFLOWER. A decoration for ballrooms.
   — A girl all dressed up and no place to glow.
Ohio State Sun Dial
   — A woe-begonia.
   — Any gal who wears a sweater merely to keep herself
     warm.   *Anon.*
   WALL STREET. The rooting section of all evil.

WAR. A racket.   *Maj. Gen. Smedley D. Butler*
— A passion play performed by idiots.   *Bill Corum*
— A most pestilential nuisance.   *George Bernard Shaw, 1917*

241

— A method of killing people, and a great many people in this world ought to be killed. *George Bernard Shaw, 1934*

— A blood-stained stagger to victory. *David Lloyd George*

— Something that knocks the "l" out of glory. *Anon.*

— Opening new markets by blasting.

— A period of intense boredom punctuated by moments of acute fear. *Seventeenth-century soldier*

— A continuation of politics by other means. *Clausewitz*

— A campaign to get more air for less people.

— An effort to extend foreign markets by killing off foreign consumers.

— War does not determine who is right—only who is left.

Montreal Star

— The application of the mechanics of force to human nature.

Gen. Douglas MacArthur

— An evil and it is often the lesser evil. Those who take the sword perish by the sword, and those who don't take the sword perish by smelly diseases. *George Orwell*

— Not popularity seeking. *Gen. William T. Sherman*

— The diplomat's vacation period. *Robert R. Young*

— A matter much too important to be left to the generals.

Georges Clemenceau

— The fertilizer business on a big scale.

WAR CORRESPONDENT. A dramatic critic who reviews fireworks.

— A man hired by a newspaper to guess what an army will do next.

WASHINGTON. The city bureauful. *G. C. Ebbert*

— The country's high-pressure point.

WASHINGTON, GEORGE. America's last Englishman and first American. *Anon.*

— A statesman who would have been the father of twins, if it hadn't been for Abraham Lincoln.

WASTE. Outgo without income.

WATCH. An imperfect approximation of the heavens.

Patek-Philippe

WATER. A colorless fluid that turns black when you wash your
   face.   *Mickey Mouse*
— A very primitive liquid.   *Henri Hery*
— Composed of two gins, Oxygin and Hydrogin. Oxygin is
   pure gin, Hydrogin is gin and water.
                            Anon., Jr. (British Division)
   HARD WATER. The scientific name for ice.   *Anon., Jr.*
   WATER WAGON. A vehicle from which a man frequently dis-
   mounts to boast of the fine ride he's having.
                                            Harry Thompson
   WATERSHED. A shed in the middle of the sea where ships
   take shelter during the middle of a storm.
                                            Anon. collegiate

WATTEAU. A British expression.   *Judge*

WAVE. A Grable-bodied seaman.   *Phil Baker*
   WAVES. The girls who go down to the sea in slips.
                                            Charlie McCarthy

WEATHER. The discourse of fools.   *English proverb*

— Every man's chatter.   *E. B. White*
   HOT WEATHER. The mother of procrastination.
                                            Thomas A. Edison
   WEATHER FORECASTING. Witchcraft by bureaucracy.

WEAVING. Tying knots to cover nudes.

WEBSTER, DANIEL. A steam engine in trousers.
                                            Sydney Smith

WEBSTER, NOAH. The author of The Right Handed Dictionary.

WEDDING. A funeral where you smell your own flowers. *Anon.*
— A ceremony in which rings are put on the finger of the lady
   and through the nose of the gentleman. *Herbert Spencer*
— Going over Niagara Falls without a barrel.
— A maternity initiation.
— A hymeneal orgy.   *H. L. Mencken*

WEDDING BELLS. A storm warning.

WEDDING CAKE. A pile of assorted millstones with a sugar coating.

WEDDING RING. A tourniquet—it stops your circulation.

Anon.

WEDGIES. Vamps on ramps.   *Macy's*

WEDLOCK. A padlock.   *English proverb*
— A situation whereby the bridegroom brings home the bacon and the bride burns it.
— The deep, deep peace of the double bed after the hurly-burly of the chaise-longue.   *Mrs. Patrick Campbell*
— What Socrates died of an overdose of.   *Anon. student*

WEED. A flower in disguise.   *James Russell Lowell*
— A plant whose virtues have not been discovered.

Ralph Waldo Emerson

WEEP. What you hit a poison wit.   *New Yorkese*

WHIP. What you do when hit by a weep.   *Ibid.*

WELLS, H. G. A writer whose history is a veritable millstone on the road to learning.   *Anon., Jr.*

WELSHER. A native of Wales.   *Anon., Jr. (British Division)*

WEST POINT. A place where the brass is polished.
  WEST POINTER. A boy who wasn't too proud to speak to a Congressman.   *Will Rogers*

WESTERN. A sage saga.
  ADULT WESTERN. One in which the hero loves his horse better than the girl, but he's worried about it.

Arthur Murray's press agents

WETNESS DAY. The fort day of the week.   *New Yorkese*

WHAT! An exclamation of disbelief, used when told the amount you will be allowed for your old car.

WHAT A YOUNG GIRL OUGHT TO KNOW. Yes.
*Morton Thompson**

WHEAT. The staff of bread.

WHEEL. The vindication of the rolling stone.

WHISKEY. The best thing to take for a headache—the night
before.   *Ed Wynn*

WHISTLE. Wind having a narrow escape.

WHITE. Beyond the pale.
  WHITE MAN. Lolema djola feka feka—the bat that flies hard
    without knowing where it is going.
Bakutu (Congo) definition

WHITE, WILLIAM ALLEN. A decayed conservative.
William Allen White

WHOA! A brake for horses.
— What Paul Revere said at the end of his famous ride.
Anon., Jr.

WHO'S WHO. A catalogue listing the highest form of livestock.

WHY? The word that invented science.
— The plural of "is," as "How why you?"   *New Yorkese*

WICKED. Anything the old cannot enjoy.   *Anton Chekhov*
  WICKEDNESS. Wholehearted sin.

WIDOW. A woman who is sadder but wiser.
— The financial remains of a love affair. *George Jean Nathan*
  GRASS WIDOW. The wife of a dead vegetarian.
Anon., Jr. (British Division)

WIFE. To tremble or waiver.   *Original meaning*
— A woman who wears nylons in zero weather—but still re-
  quires 90 per cent of the blanket.   *Lou Apuzzo*
— A housekeeper who gets bed and boredom.
— A woman who could do better if *she* were a man.

— A person who can look in the top drawer of a dresser and find a man's handkerchief that isn't there.

— A woman who, when you hear somebody in the kitchen tidying up the dishes, it's her mother. *Earl Wilson*

— A former sweetheart. *H. L. Mencken*

WILLIAMS, TENNESSEE. A writer whose plays inspire you to lie down and die.

— The nightmare merchant of Broadway. *Time*

WILL POWER. Eating only one peanut.

WIND. Weather on the go.

WINDOW. A looking-out glass.

WINDOW SCREEN. A device for keeping flies in the house.

Anon.

WINE. The divine juice of September. *Voltaire*

WINK. A whether signal. *Frank Nelson*

WINKEN, BLINKEN, AND NOD. The three wise men. *Anon., Jr.*

WINTER. The season when we try to keep the house as hot as it was in the summer, when we complained about the heat.

Anon.

WISDOM. Learning, aged in wood.

WISH. A blueprint for a dream.

WIT. The salt that makes truth palatable.

WITCH. A mother-in-law who made good. *Anon.*

— A flying sorcerer.

WIVES, AMERICAN. Women who expect to find in their husbands a perfection that English women only hope to find in their butlers. *W. Somerset Maugham*

WOLF. A man with a lot of pet theories. *Roger Williams*

— A guy who is ready, villain, and able. *Terry Moore*

WOLVES. Like railroad trains—you like to hear the whistle, even if you don't want to go any place. *Maisie*

WOMAN. The only being that can skin a wolf and get a mink.

Sam Cowling

— A perpetual emotion machine. *Frank Loesser**

— A desirable calamity. *Palladius*

— One of nature's agreeable blunders. *Hannah Cowley*

— The last thing man will civilize. *George Meredith*

— A person who thinks two and two'll make five, if she cries
and bothers enough about it. *George Eliot*

— A person who will look in a mirror any time—except when
she's pulling out of a parking space.

Atchison (Kans.) Globe

— A strange animal who can tear through an 18-inch aisle
in a crowded store, then goes home and knocks the door
off a 12-foot garage. *Cleveland Press*

— A biped with two hands, two eyes, and two faces.

*Carol Weld**

— A creature with sharp nails and a suspicious nature who
purrs when petted.

— A person who would rather have a caress than a career.

Elizabeth Marbury

— A sackful of snakes. *Ancient Arabic*

— It is easier to take care of a peck of fleas than of one
woman. *French proverb*

— An evil no household should be without. *Russian proverb*

— A multiplication table for the human species.

Nineteenth-century view

— Someone who reaches for a chair when answering the telephone. *Detroit News*

— Beneath this stone, a lump of clay,
    Lies Arabella Young,
Who on the 24th of May
    Began to hold her tongue. *Old epitaph*

— A creature between man and the angels. *Balzac*

— An afterthought of God. *Proverb*

— Woman exists chiefly to demonstrate to man the Lord's
sense of humor. *Ninon Traver Fleckenstein*

— A girl with wrinkles. *Harry Delmar**

— The animal that possesses the greatest attachment for man.

Anon., Jr.

WOMEN. The plural of whim.   *Anon. collegiate*
— The shadows of men.   *Ben Jonson*
— Poor losers.   *Anon.*
— Girls old enough to know better.
— Sphinxes without secrets.   *Oscar Wilde*
— Two classes: those who have had operations and those
  who have lost the setting from their engagement rings.
                            Jewell (Kans.) *Republican*
— The damnedest people.   *Jeeter Lester*
— Not much, but they are the best other sex we have.
                                              Don Herold
WOMEN'S INTUITION. Nothing more than man's transparency.
                                          Joseph Cossman

WOODCOCK. A husband whose wife has been untrue to him.
                                              Anon., Jr.

WOOLLCOTT, ALEXANDER. A dreamer with a fine sense of
  double-entry bookkeeping.   *Harpo Marx*

WORDS. Things to kill time until emotions make us inartic-
  ulate.   *Arthur Somers Roche*

WORK. The worst thing you can do for your health.
                                          Howard Brubaker
— The curse of the drinking classes.   *Oscar Wilde*
— A form of nervousness.   *Don Herold*

WORLD. A place on which England is found.
                                          G. K. Chesterton
— A stage, but the play is badly cast.   *Oscar Wilde*
— A pestilent congregation of vapours.   *Hamlet*
— A place that was built in six days—and looks it.
    WORLD'S FAIR. Coney Island with a collar and tie.
                                              Fred Allen
    WORLD SERIES. Competition to determine what team of
      baseball players in the upper right-hand corner of the
      U.S.A., North America, western hemisphere, the world,
      wins the most games.

WORLD-TELEGRAM. Scripps-Howard's New York show window and it looks like a J. C. Penney store in Bergdorf Goodman territory.   *A. J. Liebling*

WORLD WAR I. A historical incident that started with an assassination and ended with communism, fascism, inflation, and depression.

WORLD WAR II. The war that made the world unsafe for democracy.

WORLD WAR III. The war to eliminate the housing problem.

WORRY. Interest paid on trouble before it falls due.
                                                        Dean Inge
— A complete circle of inefficient thought revolving about a pivot of fear.   *Anon.*
— A thin stream of fear trickling through the mind. If encouraged, it cuts a channel into which all other thoughts are drained.   *Arthur Somers Roche*
— What you read between the lines of a person's face. *Grit*
— The short cut to the end of the line.   *Duke Ellington*

WRECK. Tattered cloth, i.e., "She ain't got a dissent wreck to her name."   *New Yorkese*

WRECK-IT. A thin disk you spin on a racket-player.
                                                    New Yorkese

WRESTLER. A muscle-bound comedian acting like an athlete.
   WRESTLING. The art of gripping, grappling, and griping.
   — The sport of clings.
   — Practically the only sport in which the participants groan as much as the customers.   *Judge*

WRETCHED. The long name for the nickname "Dick."
                                                Charlestonese

WRINKLE. Yesterday's dimple.   *Joseph Conrad*
— The nick of time.

WRITER. A purveyor of amusement for people who have not wit enough to entertain themselves. *George Bernard Shaw*

— One who has had an unhappy childhood.

Joseph Hergesheimer

— A man who borrows a fountain pen to autograph the flyleaf of someone else's book. *Morton Thompson**

SCENARIO WRITER. A bellboy whose view on life is a continual going up and down stairs and opening and shutting doors. *George Bernard Shaw*

WRITING. The art of putting black words on white paper in succession until the impression is created that something has been said. *Alexander Woollcott*

— A system for taking the words out of the mouth.

— The only respectable work a girl can do in bed.

Vic Fredericks

— The art of applying the seat of the pants to the seat of the chair. *Mary Heaton Vorse*

WRY-TEA. The spice of life. *New Yorkese*

X

X.   A letter which has cast its fateful shadow over everything
it has touched, down through the centuries as follows,
1,100, 200, & 69 B.C., A.C., and D.C. The glamorous Cleo-
patra, sitting in her golden barge, toying with her lilies,
would have been nowhere, practically, if it had not been
for the glamorous letter X, sitting right there alongside of
her, toying with *its* lilies.

Judas, the inventor of the Free Silver movement, produced the X-in-Spades, known to us of the cognoscenti as
the Double-X or, when applied to the lady of the house,
the Madame X.

Another way the letter X has cast its shadder on things
is like when a man comes home and finds his wife in a
plow. At this point the hired man puts his neck in a noose
and the man whips out with his Gittum and Bong! This
kind of X shows up in the newspapers the next morning
as X marks the spot and this kind of picture is invariably
crammed full of the ole X appeal.

Another way you can get the old business on X is also
out on the farm. No matter what they are selling for in
the city stores, in the country X are always ten cents a
dozen cheaper.

The most celebrated X hunt in the world's history was
staged by a guy named Diogenes, who had a long beard
over his gozzle in which he kept fresh laid X against a
time of need, as follows: Needle, needle, needle. This
Diogenes went on an X-country hunt which lasted all his
life. All he was looking for was a single blameless person.

A man with no X to grind.   *Morton Thompson**

251

X. A letter, which, though found in Saxon words, begins no word in the English language.

Dr. Samuel Johnson (before X-ray)

— The signature of a happy man.

Xmas. The five-week celebration of Thanksgiving by the gadget merchants.

X-Ray. The real inside dope.   *Frank Scully*

— A glance inside to see how the bones in the back room are doing.

Xylophone. An instrument for converting timber into timbre.

Y

YACHT RACE. The triumph of capital gains.   *Jimmy Cannon*

YALE. A period in a man's life between change of voice and
selling insurance.   *"Higher and Higher"*

YANKEE. In Europe, an American. In the northern states of
our Union, a New Englander. In the southern states the
word is unknown.   *Ambrose Bierce*
— A tourist who comes to Florida and spends his money.
                                      Mrs. Tom Ferris
  DAMNYANKEE. A tourist who comes down and stays at your
  house.   *Ibid.*

YAWN. Nature's provision for letting married men open their
mouths.   *The Burning Question*
— A reflexive play of muscles proving that criticism does not
depend upon intelligence.
— A silent shout.   *G. K. Chesterton*

YEA ILL. An obscure college in New Haven.   *Bostonese*

YEAR. A period of 365 disappointments.   *Ambrose Bierce*

YEARN. To mentally reach.

YELL (college). A commercial for amateurs.

YES MAN. One who stoops to concur.   *Greta Christiansen*

YESTERDAY. The tomorrow that got away.

YOKEL. The way people talk to each other in the Alps.
                                      Anon., Jr.
YODELING. Vocal mountain climbing.

YOM KIPPUR. A general in the Japanese army. *Anon., Jr.*

YOUNG. Certain.

YOURS TRULY. The last letter of the English alphabet.
Anon. Japanese Jr.

YOUTH. Imperfection. *Haierapolitan saying*
— A person who has a wolf in his stomach. *English proverb*
— The first fifty years of your life or the first twenty of any-
one else's. *Anon.*
— A wonderful thing; what a pity it's wasted on children.
George Bernard Shaw

YOUTHFUL FIGURE. What you get when you ask a woman her
age. *Anon.*

Z

ZEAL. The passion that goeth before a sprawl.

Ambrose Bierce

ZEBRA. A horse with stripes.

ZEPHYR. A ladylike blizzard.   *Elbert Hubbard*
— A wind that lisps.

ZIGZAG. The shortest distance between two drinks.

ZIPPER. A mechanical fly.

ZITHER. A lap harp.   *Don Quinn**
— A ukulele for quintuplets.
— A blunt instrument.

ZODIAC. The Zoo of the Sky where lions, goats, virgins, and other animals go after they are dead.   *Anon., Jr.*

ZOO. A refuge where savage beasts are protected from man.
— A place devised for animals to study the habits of human beings.   *Oliver Herford*
   ZOOLOGY. A study of life in Hollywood.
   — The scientific study of animals without the aid of the racing form.

ZULU. A tropical subject.

ZWIEBACK. Sponge cake that has lived.   *Dorothy Gulman**
— Bread with backbone.   *Ruth K. Levinson**
— The toast of the Swiss town.

ZYMURGY. The last word.   *Funk & Wagnalls*

THE END
A signal to start a sequel